PRAISE FOR *ST*

MW00643138

"If you read only one book about American higher education, read this one. *Students First* is simply the clearest, best-reasoned, and most compelling analysis of the problems facing higher education today. It is also a warning that unless we address those problems, we threaten America's most cherished hopes for social justice, economic mobility, and a robust civil society. But Paul LeBlanc offers us more than just critique; he sets out a vision and a roadmap for change based not just on glittery promises but on his hard-won experience as one of America's most innovative university presidents. Paul LeBlanc is a national treasure, and his work, in this book and on the ground, is a beacon for all of us."

> —**Ted Mitchell**, president, American Council on Education
> and former US Under Secretary of Education

"As the leading innovator in American higher education today, Paul LeBlanc paints a powerful, personal portrait of what's at stake in the urgent task of advancing social mobility through a radically redesigned system of higher education. LeBlanc makes a compelling and convincing case for a competency-based education model that will create the opportunity needed to quite literally make the world better for all of us."

> —**Jamie Merisotis**, president and CEO,
> Lumina Foundation

"In this book, Paul LeBlanc combines two scarce ingredients. The first is a loving understanding of what college students from all backgrounds need to succeed in school—not just recent high school graduates but also first-generation attenders, immigrants, working students, students who otherwise can't afford college. The second is a realistic approach to solving higher education systems problems. The result, part tough critique of today's universities, part clear-eyed and practical understanding of how to transform college accessibility, affordability, and student success, is necessary reading for anyone who wants to transform our nation's higher education systems so they are improving educational and economic opportunities for all Americans."

> —**Michael F. Bennet**, US senator and former superintendent,
> Denver Public Schools

"Colleges and universities must find ways to serve as engines of opportunity, particularly for first-generation college students, working adults, and others who can't afford to attend a residential campus for four or more years. LeBlanc's book offers a bold proposal for addressing access, equity, and quality of actual learning, while rethinking federal financial aid to better support low-income learners. A must-read for anyone interested in making higher education once again work for everyone, not just the privileged."

> —**Arne Duncan**, former US Secretary of Education

"*Students First* is a wonderful book. Written by one of the country's most thoughtful and successful educators, this is a volume that succeeds in telling stories of both dreams and despair, documenting the problems higher education faces and offering visionary and pragmatic solutions for the future. It is one of those rare and very readable books that pulls no punches but leaves the reader with a feeling of optimism about tomorrow. It's a must-read for anyone who works in or cares about the future of higher education."

—**Arthur Levine**, president emeritus, Teachers College, Columbia University; senior fellow, Institute for Citizens and Scholars (formerly Woodrow Wilson National Fellowship Foundation); and distinguished scholar of higher education, Steinhardt Institute of Higher Education Policy, New York University

"Paul LeBlanc breaks new ground with this compelling case for competency-based higher education. Leveraging deep expertise and lived experience, *Students First* is a critical contribution to the debate around the future of higher education, and it could not come at a more important time."

—**Maria Flynn**, president and CEO, Jobs for the Future

"For higher education, a pressing challenge is access: with the tools at hand, how do we do more to unlock talent that for too long has remained hidden? Through his inspired, innovative, and pragmatic leadership, President LeBlanc continues to find fresh answers, transforming SNHU into an engine of opportunity along the way. His optimism, energy, and clarity of thought leap from the pages of this important work."

—**L. Rafael Reif**, president, Massachusetts Institute of Technology

"In this book, Paul LeBlanc uses his invaluable experience as an innovator in higher education to share a path forward for America's higher education system as a tool for deeper human understanding and for equity and access to all learners at every stage of their education and careers. LeBlanc's compelling argument—that higher education's focus on outmoded, time-based measures of achievement is rendering it increasingly irrelevant in the twenty-first century—should serve as an important spark to start a long-overdue conversation. And should help us achieve real, measurable progress."

—**Maggie Hassan**, former governor of New Hampshire

"This important book—from one of America's most innovative university presidents—dares us to rethink higher education on what seem to be the most sensible notions: let's focus on actual learning and let's make learning work for each individual learner. But higher education is built around deeply flawed measures of time and treats all students with the misguided benchmark of the 'average learner.' There is no such learner, and our systems fail far too many. LeBlanc offers a bold Plan B, one rooted in real-world experience, tested and proven, and available to us if we are courageous enough to embrace it."

—**Todd Rose**, author, The End of Average; coauthor, Dark Horse; and cofounder, Populace

"Both K–12 education and higher education will become truly centered on student learning and smoothly integrated when they flip from a tired model of 'time served' to align around 'competencies earned.' LeBlanc does us all a favor, laying out this vision and how we can get there faster. Read *Students First* and sign on—our future depends on it."

—**Chris Gabrieli**, chairman of the board,
Massachusetts Department of Higher Education

"For all those concerned about the teaching and learning at colleges and universities, this is the book that's needed now, written by the right person to point the way forward. Paul LeBlanc lays out the challenges and opportunities for colleges to play a meaningful role in every individual's development in prose that is relatable and clear. The conclusion from the book is clear as well: it's past time to rethink our time-based education system to focus on learning."

—**Michael B. Horn**, coauthor, Choosing College, Disrupting Class, and Blended and cofounder, Clayton Christensen Institute

"Even before the pandemic, there was an urgent need for a radical rethink in higher education to ensure it matched students' aspirations and set them up to succeed in the economy and society of the future. The pandemic has intensified the importance and urgency of the task. Paul LeBlanc's book explains how it can be done. In addition to being well written and well argued, the book has the great virtue that the author has not just thought deeply about the challenges involved; he has overcome them in practice and actually done what he says needs to be done. Not just theory. Not just practice. Both."

—**Sir Michael Barber**, founder and chair,
Delivery Associates

"'President Paul LeBlanc, you saved my life,' a student whispers as she walks across the stage during an SNHU graduation. This is what we want for everyone. This book not only shows what our education system is missing, how it costs too much and is inequitable, but shows us the way Paul has broken through barriers towards a more equitable and affordable competency-based college. *Students First* is a historical analysis of a problem, but more importantly it outlines a way forward. The journey should inspire us all to be our own pioneers of change for our students. It is a book I will give to all of my staff to read."

—**Dennis Littky**, cofounder, Big Picture Learning and cofounder,
Metropolitan Regional Career and Technical Center

"In this text Paul LeBlanc argues powerfully for a long-overdue rethink of higher education. Whilst deeply embedded in the US higher education world, this book has powerful lessons for higher education everywhere. If we don't think about how our students, and future students, engage with the world and if we are not relevant to their lived experiences, then the higher education system will begin to become less relevant and be overtaken. Paul argues for profound change in the way that we build higher education in order that we serve industry and commerce, our students, and society with the opportunities that they deserve. Paul presents this text from a deeply personal perspective: he has done it and done it brilliantly. We should all listen."

—**Ian Dunn**, provost, Coventry University

"To know how upside-down the priorities of higher 'education' are, you need only know that the football coach at Clemson made $8.3 million last year as part of a ten-year, $93 million contract, while tens of thousands of higher education students are failing to complete their degrees each year because of systemic failings. SNHU president, leading higher education innovator, and author Paul LeBlanc knows this absurdity well and, at SNHU, he has put his money where his mouth is by building scaled delivery of competency-based online higher education where the priority is the 150,000-plus global students. As absurd as it is for an 'amateur' college football coach to have a $93 million contract, in this important new book, Paul successfully asserts the equivalent absurdity of a higher education system that tethers students to grading curves and seat time rather than standards of learning and mastery that would equip all students for personal and economic success."

—**Deborah Quazzo**, managing partner,
GSV Ventures and cofounder, ASU+GSV Summit

"This is a book of great consequence—brilliant clarity on why and how higher education has gone off track, and how to transform it. Students First is a recipe for reforming higher education and bettering the lives of millions of people—Dr. Paul LeBlanc is the master chef."

—**Matthew Wunder**, CEO and cofounder,
Da Vinci Schools

"Paul LeBlanc extends a provocative invitation to deconstruct higher education and rethink its role in the dawn of a new era for learning. Here's the why and how formal HE institutions should lead in times of disruption. A must-read for the optimistic and the bold who believe this is the most exciting time for education, and for those ready to join Paul in his visionary quest to fulfill the needs of each learner."

—**Nieves Segovia**, president,
SEK Education Group

STUDENTS
FIRST

STUDENTS FIRST

Equity, Access, and Opportunity
in Higher Education

With gratitude

Paul

PAUL LeBLANC

HARVARD EDUCATION PRESS

Cambridge, Massachusetts

Copyright © 2021 by the President and Fellows of Harvard College

All rights reserved. No part of this publication may be reproduced or transmitted in any form or by any means, electronic or mechanical, including photocopy, recording, or any information storage and retrieval systems, without permission in writing from the publisher.

Paperback ISBN 978-1-68253-675-9

Library of Congress Cataloging-in-Publication data is on file.

Published by Harvard Education Press,
an imprint of the Harvard Education Publishing Group

Harvard Education Press
8 Story Street
Cambridge, MA 02138

Cover Design: Ciano Design
Cover Photo: naqiewei/DigitalVision Vectors via Getty Images

The typefaces used in this book are Candide, D Sari, and ITC Century.

For our students,
who deserve our best.

CONTENTS

FOREWORD

Reinventing American Higher Education for a New World Order

LONG BEFORE THE PANDEMIC upended the world, it was not an under-statement to remark that American higher education is under fire. Yes, COVID-19 has had dramatic effects on education—and we continue to feel the repercussions—but what became visible during a time of turmoil are issues that have long been simmering near the surface. The foundational questions of "What is a college education?" and "Is college worthwhile?" received heightened attention as institutions scrambled to create new models in the face of an uncertain pandemic. However, these are core questions higher education has been grappling with for years. An increas-ing number of headlines and public conversations underscore growing mistrust of postsecondary institutions and whether the high price of many colleges and universities is justified.

The concerns and criticisms facing colleges and universities are numerous. Some suggest students are not learning critical skills that are relevant for today's workforce. In addition, as data have become more available, along with the ability to track students over time and across institutions, it has become clear that completion rates in American higher education are weak overall and dismal for some groups of students. In fact, even among graduates, there is growing variation in outcomes—while the average return to getting a college degree is positive and robust, there are a growing number of students who fall far below the mean to a level that suggests they are attaining little value. Beyond the benefits to individuals, there are also questions about the public returns to higher education with doubts about whether institutions are serving societal needs and are deserving of the government subsidies they receive either in direct form (i.e., state appropriations to public institutions) and/or through tax exemption (public and nonprofit private institutions). At every turn, colleges and universities are facing skepticism, and the public no longer takes on faith that higher education is worth the cost.

I write this as someone who has benefited from the best our system has to offer, with opportunities to grow in a multitude of ways, and my research for the past twenty-five years has focused on identifying and improving the good that is done by colleges and universities to support and advance students, especially those from low-income backgrounds. Still, while the United States has some of the best institutions in the world, it also fails to serve large numbers of students. And so, this was the backdrop as American higher education began to experience the effects of COVID-19.

It was around the first wave of impacts felt from the pandemic, in April 2020, that I participated in a webinar with Paul LeBlanc, which was hosted by my institution, the Harvard Graduate School of Education. Paul has been a longtime innovator in higher education, leading Southern New Hampshire University (SNHU) to become a powerful force and example in online education, in addition to its campus programs focused on traditional college students. At a time when many colleges and universities were forced to dismantle their usual models (and students were often responding quite unfavorably), Paul provided a seasoned perspective on how institutions could navigate the challenges, adapt in the face of evolving conditions, and address the inequities being experienced by students. It was a timely conversation, but at the root of it, the issues we discussed were about higher education's future more generally, and it is wonderful to see many of those ideas now represented in this book. As higher education confronts increased scrutiny and doubt in the midst of continuing uncertainty, Paul's insights are sorely needed.

Beyond the debates about the value of higher education and the criticisms listed above, a much more pernicious concern relates to a core function of colleges and universities: fostering students' learning. Are students learning? Better yet, are they learning the critical skills and knowledge to make a meaningful wage and be productive members of society? Unfortunately, efforts to develop indicators on learning have been slow, incomplete, and suffered setbacks as there have been attempts to bring them to scale. The constant struggle—and at time inability—to measure learning is closely tied to the inadequate measures we default to when discussing college quality. It is quite telling that the predominate measure of college "quality" draws from the *U.S. News and World Report* rankings—notable for the fact that the bulk of the measures used focus on achievement that happened before the student ever stepped foot on campus (i.e., test scores and grades in high school). While those data may give some sense of the prior achievement levels of the student body, they do not reflect the ability of an institution to foster the growth of a student.

Perhaps this partly explains how our higher education system came to be built on a foundation that counts time, not learning. As Paul explains from the first page of chapter 1, the emphasis on credit hours, i.e., units of time, is a major fault for our current model of higher education. With clear insight, Paul discusses the many ways this system is problematic as a means to gauge student progress. This is especially true in a world with increasingly diverse students and mobility across institutions. During the past several decades, the number of students who are nontraditional in some way—older, part-time, concurrently employed, veterans, parents, and so on—has grown substantially. Students are also more likely to have disrupted patterns of attendance (i.e., stopping out and returning to college at a later time) and to attend multiple institutions. Also important is the fact that students are much more likely to have work experience to couple with their postsecondary studies, leading to questions about how to credit them for the knowledge and skills they bring with them to class. The changes we see in higher education necessitate a new model— one that goes beyond the simple reliance on credit hours and the narrow conception of a college student being a recent high school graduate who attends college full time.

A related concern of importance is affordability. The list price of higher education has skyrocketed and now is far out of reach for most families. And with growing debt, concerns about affordability may be the crack that ultimately causes a dramatic change in the higher education system. Like so much else, financial aid is awarded based on credit hours, which keeps it disconnected from actual learning or growth. Paul presents an alternative by describing a system that provides financial support based on completing competencies, thus better aligning actions that would improve students' skills with the goals of taxpayers. With his attention to the necessary details, Paul's discussion of this important issue is a strength of the book and demonstrates a strong combination of the practical and the aspirational—both are needed to improve our system.

While I could continue detailing the challenges facing higher education and concerns about what needs to change, this is definitely not the time to give up on the system. To the contrary, there is incredible urgency in the importance of moving toward a better system. The opportunity to learn and ability to gain skills have become even more important to the life outcomes of individuals, and as a nation, the social benefits to education are critical to having flourishing families, communities, and economies. That is why this book is so timely and important. Beyond just interrogating the problems, Paul does the much more difficult task of developing and discussing implementation of a set of possible solutions.

Interestingly, some of his recommendations seem even more feasible and promising after a year experimenting with new modes of instructional delivery and types of student engagement and support. In fact, the aftermath of COVID-19 may bring higher education to a full-on reckoning. What was once hypothetical became real out of necessity during a year when campuses were forced to change their default conditions.

Meanwhile, questions about whether colleges and universities are teaching the right content became practical dilemmas for institutions needing to pivot their teaching. Starting afresh, many professors revisited the central question of course design: what are the learning goals? Moreover, in new formats, there had to be consideration for how we were going to measure whether actual learning was happening. So the shock to the higher education system caused by COVID-19 may have helped to focus institutions on the important issues that need to be considered in reimaging what the system could be. Indeed, necessity is the mother of invention, and the ideas presented in this book provide a helpful blueprint.

Bridget Terry Long
April 2021

PREFACE

MY FAMILY IMMIGRATED to the United States in 1960 from a hardscrabble farming village in the Canadian Maritimes. We settled in the south side of Waltham, Massachusetts, just two blocks from the old Waltham Watch factory, in a melting pot neighborhood of diverse ethnic backgrounds and multifamily homes. My father worked in construction as a mason, my mother in a factory as a stitcher making car tops. They often picked up extra income cleaning offices and homes. I remember learning English and how to read in the study of a beautiful home in Weston, Boston's wealthiest suburb, sitting in a window seat with the sounds of vacuuming and my mother's soft singing as backdrop. My parents had eighth-grade educations, which was common then in rural Canada, and no one in our large extended family had ever attended college. College was reserved for children who lived in homes like the ones my mother cleaned. An unthinkable option for people like us.

My mother vividly remembered the conversation that changed every-thing, both for her and me. Mark Schlafman was my sixth-grade teacher at Ezra C. Fitch Elementary School. I remember Mr. Schlafman because he was good friends with my idol, Celtics player and legend John Havlicek, and because he later became an NBA referee. What my mother recalled about Mr. Schlafman was the parent-teacher meeting in which he said to her, "You know, Paul could go to college." This idea seems hardly pro-found today, but it was the very first time that option, however remote and still years away, had been raised. It was the conversation that lifted us from poverty of aspiration.

Fast forward more than forty years and skip ahead a generation to my daughters, Emma and Hannah. Their parents are college graduates and professionals. Children of an English professor turned college pres-ident, they grew up on college campuses. College was not a distant pos-sibility—it was an immediate reality. And the question was *where* they'd attend, not *if*. Both attended highly selective undergraduate programs. Emma recently finished her doctor of philosophy at the University of Oxford and is off to Yale Law School. Hannah completed her doctorate at Stanford University and is in a post-doc at Cal Tech. With a lot of hard work, some smarts, a fair bit of privilege, and a little luck, they have and should continue to have rewarding and meaningful work and lives. Their grandmother remained immensely proud (probably to the chagrin of her retirement home neighbors, regaled with stories of her granddaughters) until she passed away at age ninety-six, even as she could scarcely imag-ine the lives led by the granddaughters who adored her.

How does one trace the line from my parents' humble backgrounds to my daughters' walking the hallowed halls of Oxford and Stanford? The source of this social mobility, the bridge between the starkly different experiences of my parents and my children, was my education. The men-toring of wonderful public-school teachers like Mr. Schlafman led me to Massachusetts state colleges, first Westfield State University (then College) and then Framingham State University (also a college at the time). I was able to mostly pay for my college costs by working construction in the summers and having a work-study job during the school year, graduating and social mobility for its children that I enjoyed when my family came to this country in 1960. Racism (I enjoyed the advantage of being white), limited employment opportunities, and a drop in the real earnings from the minimum wages those jobs often pay all further hinder social mobility. A 2017 study published in *Science* showed that only half of those born in 1984 are doing economically better than their parents.[10] David Grusky, a Stanford sociologist and coauthor of the study says, "A big part of the American dream is that each generation will do better than the one that preceded it. That has been part of what's supposed to make this country special and distinctive. When it's just a coin flip, we're not living up to that commitment. It's a pretty fundamental part of what we say this country can deliver and we're not."

At the heart of the American myth is the notion that one's future and identity are not defined by one's social status at birth. In "The Land of Opportunity" a person can make of themselves what they wish. We have deep cultural attachment to Horatio Alger rags-to-riches stories, whether an Oprah Winfrey born into rural poverty, Howard Schultz growing up in the projects, or Sam Walton leaving the family farm in Oklahoma to create the world's largest retail business. Sometimes those success stories include dropping out of college—as Bill Gates and Larry Ellison both did—but those are exceptions that prove the rule.

The great engine of social mobility in the American success story has been higher education. And the creation of the GI Bill in 1944 democratized college and fueled a period of unprecedented economic growth and prosperity, though not for Black Americans, it is important to note. Higher education expanded and offered an affordable option for almost anyone who wanted to enroll. Americans developed a bedrock belief in the power of college to unlock opportunity and to secure a higher standard of living. With education, the child of the factory worker could become the business owner whose child would become a lawyer or a doctor, and each generation would be better off than the one that came before.

That myth has been shattered. After decades of little to no real improvement in earnings and the shock of the Great Recession, many Americans are not at all certain that their children will do better than they did. Confidence in higher education has declined significantly in the US since 2015, Gallup has found, more so than for any other domestic institution Gallup tracks.[11] And while employers generally are confident in higher education, they tend to think recent graduates are better prepared to succeed in entry-level positions than to advance in their jobs.[12] Employers also say colleges and universities need to make changes to ensure that graduates have the skills and knowledge needed for the workforce.

While we ask higher education to do many important things—conduct research and expand knowledge, create better citizens and enrich culture, and support economic growth—most families want three things from college:

- the right credential to unlock the door to a successful career (and success means some combination of good pay, meaningful work, and a stable future)
- for it to be affordable
- to make students feel as though they matter, providing a sense of belonging and that institutions genuinely care about them

When taken together, the first two items define the *value* of higher education for most people. The third item defines the industry's relationship to the American public. Higher education is not doing nearly as well as it needs to on all three fronts, and some would argue that it is contributing to the nation's discontent and widening inequities.

An influential trove of research from Harvard University's Opportunity Insights captures just how successful—or not—colleges are at helping students reach higher wage brackets after graduation.[13] These "mobility rates" aren't pretty for many institutions, including those that have plenty of resources to do better. Many campuses in the City University of New York system have upward mobility rates that are three times higher than the average rates for the Ivy League and other highly selective private institutions as well as for flagship public universities. And despite the broad push for college access in recent decades, the research shows that low-income students on average are much more likely to be shut out of high-mobility colleges that can help them make it to the middle class.

This book is rooted in my own story, my unshakable belief that education remains the greatest force for social good that we have available to us, and my growing conviction that the American higher education system that worked so well for decades and became the envy of the world is failing today. It is my attempt to reimagine higher education for what some have called the Fourth Industrial Age, one in which most of us will have algorithmic coworkers; where digital and physical realities blend; where the speed of change continues to accelerate; where our ethical, political, and social systems struggle to keep up; and where we entertain unprecedented opportunities for both great good and great evil.

Higher education as an industry is in many ways ill-suited for this new reality. It is too slow, too rigidly hierarchal and territorial, too hesitant to adopt new technologies and ways of doing things, too inefficient, and too focused on itself. We need a higher education *ecosystem* through which people will move in and out over the course of their careers and lives. It would as easily accommodate a tenth-grade girl working on college math as a sixty-five-year-old formerly incarcerated man finishing a high school diploma. Degrees would remain important milestones, but learning could also be just-in-time and more dynamic. Rather than the fragmented and generally disconnected approach we have today, we need a coherent, interconnected system for learning that can provide just the right learning at just the right time in just the right way. Such an ecosystem would harness technology to accommodate more learning pathways, include more providers beyond colleges and universities, provide a greater range and granularity of credentials, and offer much more flexibility and individualization than is possible today. Such a system needs to rethink its use of time-based structures of learning, with all the inequities they carry for people who have too little time.

A 2020 report from the Brookings Institution describes the growing "middle class time squeeze," which has been driven by an uneven distribution of time demands.[14] "Time is the ultimate scarcity," the researchers write. "Not only do Americans work longer hours than those in other advanced nations, but the gap in longevity between those with higher and lower incomes has widened in the U.S." As solutions, the report calls for better alignment of schedules for education and work as well as the creation of subsidized lifelong learning accounts people can use to pay for education when they need it. Central to this book's argument is the idea that an education system built on structures and measures of time is poorly equipped to assess actual student learning, too rigid and thus unresponsive to the fast-changing world in which we live, and increasingly inequitable for the growing portion of the American public for which time is neither abundant nor flexible.

Much of the change underway in higher education is painful. But this book is optimistic. We can innovate and rethink what we do to better serve society. Most importantly, I'm not worried about all college students. For plenty of fortunate students, those like my daughters, the system works well enough. I'm concerned about students of all ages from lower- and middle-socioeconomic classes who face an uncertain future. They need something different from higher education. Not lesser, but better suited for their lives. And growing inequity makes this imperative even more urgent. The discussion that follows may raise more questions than it answers. But my hope is that it can help institutions and stakeholders develop higher-quality, lower-cost educational pathways to keep the American Dream alive for this next generation of students, who are not much different and no less deserving than I was when higher education changed my life.

CHAPTER ONE

LEAVING AMERICANS BEHIND

The Problem of Time and the Credit Hour

MARIAN WASN'T READY FOR COLLEGE when I first met her. She was in her late twenties and had tried college before, taking courses at two community colleges in Boston. Her transcripts were riddled with Fs and withdrawals. The odds were heavily stacked against her earning a college degree.

The single mother of a ten-year-old daughter with chronic respiratory problems, Marian lived in one of Boston's poorest neighborhoods and had little family support, hardly any money, and almost no time. She often had to stay home to care for her daughter, missing a week or more of classes. She would fall behind, turning in assignments late and struggling with exams—or missing them altogether—and her grades showed it. Because Marian's college courses, like almost all college courses, required her to be at a set place at a set time, she was forced to choose between her daughter's care and class attendance. Her studies suffered greatly, and she was using up her federal financial aid. Marian continued to fail, and she was on the verge of joining the thirty-seven million Americans who have some college credits and student debt, but no degree.

Time was the problem. Marian was poor and that means everything takes more time. Without a washer and dryer, having clean clothes takes longer. Without a car, getting groceries takes longer. Without good medical insurance, getting seen by a health-care professional often means longer wait times.

Being poor also means having less control of your time. For example, fast-food workers rarely work set schedules and must be on the job at times that can change on a weekly or even daily basis. That unpredictability makes it nearly impossible for them to manage childcare and a myriad of daily tasks that wealthier Americans can manage with predictable, flexible work schedules.

The millions of Americans who are enrolled in college while holding down full-time jobs and taking care of families often struggle to find set times for their studies, opening textbooks during lunch breaks at work or late at night after their kids are finally in bed. This is partially why working students tend to dislike group learning projects so much, because they are too overscheduled to commit to regular meetings with their fellow students. When lower-income working students drop out of our programs, we in higher education often say, "Life got in the way." What we often mean is that some new demand interfered with their ability to be in class at a set time each week, the way Marian's daughter's periodic illness interrupted her studies. Like so many others, Marian was ready to give up.

Marian's college experience was hardly exceptional. Despite the national fixation on high-priced colleges with lavish residence halls, nationally ranked football teams, and selective admissions, that vision of higher education is not a reality for the vast majority of students. Just 15 percent of US undergraduates attend residential colleges. And while most people think the majority of college freshman live on a campus, only 13 percent of them do, according to a 2018 report from Higher Learning Advocates.[1] More than 80 percent of students commute to campus or attend online. And about 45 percent of all undergraduates are enrolled at community college. Like Marian, 43 percent of full-time students work while attending college.[2] Among part-time students, 81 percent hold down jobs, with 47 percent working at least thirty-five hours per week. Policy makers and the journalists who write about higher education are almost always from the small slice of the population that attended a traditional, residential campus, which skews our political and public discourse about the industry.

Being anchored to a rigid course and term schedule (and a physical campus) didn't give Marian the flexibility her time-starved life required. The higher education system she encountered wasn't built for her—it was built for its own organizational needs, such as how to schedule instructors and classrooms, and how to distribute financial aid. Our higher education system now works best for a small fraction of the nation's student population.

I have been president of Southern New Hampshire University since 2003. The university's online programs have made it one of the nation's largest universities, now serving more than 170,000 learners, more than twice the face-to-face enrollment of any US campus. A key reason for the popularity of SNHU's online degree programs is that they provide students with more flexibility. While still working within the framework of a set term, the university requires no standard class time online—an asynchronous model. A note for the uninitiated: *synchronous* learning requires students to meet in class at set times, while *asynchronous* learning allows them to log onto courses whenever they like. In our asynchronous model, students can complete their work when it best suits their schedule. With traditional colleges, a student might work all day, race to a campus for a class (maybe just grabbing a snack on the way), and, if lucky, get home in time to see her kids before their bedtime. In our online classes, that student can work all day, race instead to see a child play in a soccer match, have dinner with her family, and then, after tucking the kids into bed, log on and become a student.

That kind of flexibility works well for working adults, sometimes called nontraditional students, and millions of them have migrated to online degree programs. However, time flexibility is also important for many traditional-age students (eighteen- to twenty-four-year-olds). A growing

number of younger college students also work, have family responsibilities, and suffer a paucity of time. SNHU now enrolls more than thirty thousand traditional-age students in its online and campus-based programs.

THE CARNEGIE UNIT AND TIME IN SEATS

Time, not learning, largely shapes our model of higher education. We
use measures of time to mark student progress—naming each 25-percent
increment on the way to a bachelor's degree with *freshman, sophomore,
junior,* and *senior.* The length or term of each course is some number of
weeks set on the calendar. Students have course schedules that tell them
when to be in class. We assign a final grade at the end of the term, a fixed
moment in time, usually exam week, that pays no regard to the capacity
or circumstances of individual learners. We use a measure of time (and
ostensibly learning), a construct called the *credit hour,* as a foundation for
higher education.

Bear with me for a brief exploration of how this flawed measuring
unit came to be, how it contributes to many of the industry's ills, and how
the time is ripe to move to a better standard. It's important to understand
the backstory of this relatively technical measurement of time, which per-
meates higher education and how we structure it, even defining student
success. As we shall see, the limitations of the credit hour have resulted
in a system of inputs, often prescribed and with no measurable impact on
the actual quality of education. Instead, I will argue for a higher education
system built on outcomes—what a student actually knows and can do as
a result of their education.

The credit hour is like higher education's Higgs boson particle, the
elementary building block in quantum physics that helps hold the uni-
verse together. We use the credit hour to define milestones of progress
(freshman = 0 to 30 credit hours; sophomore = 30 to 60; junior = 60 to 90;
senior = 90 to 120), to set student schedules (typically 15 credit hours or five
3-credit-hour courses in a semester), to assign classrooms (a 3-credit-hour
course typically requires the use of a classroom for 150 to 180 minutes

each week), to assign faculty workloads (how many 3-credit-hour courses an instructor teaches in a term), and to declare when a student has now become a college graduate (usually at the completion of 120 credit hours, no matter how well or how poorly they have performed). We send tuition bills calculated on the basis of cost per credit hour. While we sometimes say the credit hour measures "seat time," it really is meant to measure *expected* "academically engaged time," which can include laboratories, studio work, internships, and group projects outside of class. Credit-hour expectations have little bearing on student realities, and no institution accurately measures student compliance. For example, my college roommate hardly studied for his science courses and always got an A. I put in many, many hours only to get a C. For all the energy that regulators and institutions put into credit-hour definitions and expectations, it is a woefully inadequate and inaccurate measure of actual student work.

The credit hour is also the basis for awarding more than $120 billion in federal financial aid each year through Title IV of the Higher Education Act of 1965.[3] That enormous sum of money includes federal Pell Grants, which are designed to help very poor students (usually with annual family incomes of less than $20,000); grant programs; and subsidized and unsubsidized federal loans. It provides qualified students with financial assistance for tuition and the cost of attending college, which can include books, a laptop, gas money, and more. Federal financial aid makes college possible for millions of Americans and provides much of the revenue for higher education institutions. Its availability and disbursement are greatly defined by time, as reflected in complex, time-related rules having to do with satisfactory academic progress; definitions of the academic year, term, and credit hour; and lifetime limits on Pell Grant eligibility based on time (six full academic years of program study).

In addition, we use the credit hour as the one agreed-upon measure of student learning across higher education, alongside grades. In other words, we have built an entire postsecondary education system not on the basis of actual education or student learning, but on an arbitrary construct of time that has almost no relationship to learning. But the credit hour was never meant to play this role. In her superb 2012 report, *Cracking the Credit Hour,* Amy Laitinen offers the best history of the credit hour and reminds us of the modest goal of its origin. Andrew Carnegie, then a trustee at Cornell University, sought to create a free pension system for professors that required a standard measure of time, what is sometimes called the "Carnegie Unit," which we know as the credit hour. As Laitinen, director for higher education with the Education Policy program at New America, writes:

> *Using the Carnegie Unit as a model, it was determined that faculty members who taught 12 credit units, with each unit equal to one hour of faculty-student contact time per week over a 15-week semester, would qualify for full-time pension benefits. Soon, what became known as the "credit hour" would become the fundamental building block of college courses and degree programs.*[4]

The credit hour was never envisioned as a measure of learning or academic quality. Yet it lent itself so well to the administration of colleges—everything from billing to record keeping to facility management—that it became the core organizational element of institutional operations, and thus the student experience, including the measurement of learning.

Yet time is a terrible proxy for learning. It's easy to use and apply broadly, especially compared to attempting to actually measure the quality and quantity of student learning. However, using time as the standard for measurement means our system is essentially built on *how long a student sits in class.* A typical college degree certifies that a graduate has sat through forty three-credit courses. A transcript records what courses they completed and the grades they earned. But it doesn't show what the student genuinely learned. An employer looking at the transcript of a recent graduate who took a managerial accounting course might infer what topics were covered and accept that her passing grade suggests she did well. Not much additional insight is offered, and the employer can make no trustworthy assessment of what she actually knows about managerial accounting or what skills she gained from the course.

Most of us who were fortunate enough to attend a traditional college remember at least one course where many of our classmates (and sometimes we) dialed it in by skipping classes and assignments. Think about the large lecture courses most colleges offer, usually of the introductory, 101 variety. Many of the seats remain empty in those classes, even at the most rigorous of colleges. And slacking students often slide by, failing to master required learning along the way. But a potential employer's HR department can't tell in any meaningful way what the graduate knows and can do. Or what they don't know. And because our-time based system only attempts to measure a snapshot of knowledge at a particular moment, we can't tell much about what a student retained from that Western civ class they took years ago. The credit hour isn't designed to perform those functions and has little use outside of an institution's own bureaucratic workings.

WHAT ABOUT GRADES?

A reasonable reader might ask what grades show about student achievement. Don't they at least reflect some level of learning? Shouldn't they help show what a student can do on the job?

The fact is that grades provide very little useful information, mostly indicating that students with A grades performed better than those with B grades, that those students performed better than those with C grades, and so on. That relative scaling of performance happens within the singular instance of a course (in a large university there may be many sections of the same course taught at the same time by different faculty members). The grade indicates nowhere what students learned and is often based on poor assessment practices. Moreover, as many studies have shown, we live in an age of rampant grade inflation. Half of all undergraduate grades today are As, as Laitinen notes, compared to only 15 percent in 1961.[5] The bottom line is that grades fail to show much if they are meant to signify learning across some measure of time, typically the end of a three-credit-hour course or fifteen weeks.

Universities do not trust grades, either. When students seek to transfer from one institution to another, they provide their new institution with a transcript. But because learning, teaching, and rigor are so variable; grades so untrustworthy; and perceived institutional quality so uneven, universities are often reluctant to grant full credit for the learning that students have done at other institutions. For the 37 percent of students who transfer between colleges at least once,[6] this failure to fully count credit hours adds considerable cost to the completion of a degree, often for those who can ill afford it.

As Michael Horn and Richard Price wrote in a recent essay, transfer students typically lose 43 percent of the credits they bring with them.[7] That is, the new institution refuses to accept those credits, and students lose ground while paying more for their degrees. Transfer students in California pay on average "an extra $36,000 for their bachelor's degrees, if they can get them at all," Horn and Price noted. And because so many college students receive federal financial aid, millions of dollars of taxpayer support are lost or wasted in the inefficiency of the transfer credit "system," if we can really call it a system at all.

Other factors contribute to the woeful state of credit transfer. Program requirements for a major at one college may be quite different than those for the same major at another institution. And some amount of arrogance is certainly at play—*the intro-to-psychology course at the community college across town surely can't be as good as ours*—as institutions and faculty jealously monitor the formal and informal pecking orders of status that are rife in higher education. When receiving institutions accept more transfer credits, students need fewer courses to complete their studies, reducing the amount of tuition dollars collected by the institution. Similarly, when faculty accept more transfer credits, they decrease enrollments in the courses they want to offer. In both cases, there is a financial disincentive to accept transfer credits. For their part, students often make poor decisions about what courses to take, in part because they typically lack access to good advising, and then discover those courses aren't valued or counted at their new institution. Most of those problems could be overcome if we had a well-defined measure of student learning that everyone could understand and trust. The credit hour is not that measure.

Grades also have more fundamental problems. When assigning a grade at the end of a course, we are making time *fixed* and learning a *variable*. Time is the nonnegotiable—the course ends when the course ends—and there is no across-the-board consistency of student learning. In other words, we rigidly commit to time but not to a high standard of student learning. The old student jokes that "D still gets the degree" and "C stands for completed" mean we routinely confer degrees on students who have performed poorly in their courses. (And those are Cs and Ds amid rampant grade inflation!) It is telling that graduate programs, with their greater rigor, often accept as passing no course grade lower than a B. I was an English major in college. For the math requirement, the university offered a course called *Math for Poets*, which was designed for math-challenged students like me. But even with that easier approach, I only managed to pass. As a result, I graduated with a dire lack of quantitative skills. It was only years later, when I had to manage budgets in increasingly complex managerial roles, that I mastered those competencies.

I often speak to rooms full of business executives and ask them to raise their hands if they have hired graduates of elite colleges who can't write well. Invariably, every hand in the room goes up. The same is true if I ask about quantitative skills or critical thinking. Three or four decades ago, a college degree was a signal to the labor market that a graduate was generally capable. That signal is no longer trusted by employers. A much-quoted 2014 Gallup survey found that 96 percent of college provosts described their institutions as "very or somewhat" effective at preparing students for the world of work.[8] But just 11 percent of business leaders strongly agreed that college graduates have the skills and competencies needed by their workplaces. This is a significant mismatch because most students want a college degree so they can get a well-paying job.

About half of first-year students arrive at college unprepared to do college-level math or writing. And if Richard Arum and Josipa Roksa's 2011 book, *Academically Adrift: Limited Learning on College Campuses*, is accurate, more than a third of them will be no better off at the end of four years.[9] The credit-hour system means that when a student graduates, we can be certain about how long they sat in class, but not what they've actually learned. The concern extends well beyond the skills we associate with the workplace, to include the critical thinking and civics knowledge critical to a well-functioning democracy. The baseless charges about a stolen presidential election that led to the storming of the US Capitol on January 6, 2021; the proliferation of conspiracy theories such as QAnon; science denial around the pandemic, vaccines, and climate change—often promulgated by graduates of our most elite universities—suggest a massive failure of education in the United States.

I once questioned student learning under our credit-hour system while speaking on a panel with another university president, who led a nonselective public university in a neighboring state. She vehemently disagreed, saying all graduates of her university could write well. I know some of her graduates. They aren't all capable writers. I often cringe when I see the writing of some of SNHU's about-to-graduate seniors. And when my peers are being honest about their students, they do too. It's true that our K–12 system is passing along too many high school graduates who are not ready for college-level work. But our postsecondary institutions double down on the problem because, like high schools, we measure student achievement by time served and unreliable grades. Time is fixed, learning is variable.

Another problem with time as a measure of student learning is that it depends on the concept of an average student. Final grades are based on ill-defined assumptions about how such an average student should perform over a set amount of time, the term. Lower grades are below the average and high grades above. Yet as Todd Rose points out in *The End of Average*, the very idea of "average" is deeply flawed. There is no average student.[10] Rose debunks a generally held assumption that someone who learns faster is a better learner or smarter than someone who requires a different pace or more time. In reviewing the work of educational researcher Benjamin Bloom, Rose wrote

> *Bloom showed that when students were allowed a little flexibility in the pace of their learning, the vast majority of students ended up*

performing extremely well. . . . These two insights—that speed does not equal ability, and that there are no universally fast or slow learners—had actually been recognized several decades before Bloom's pioneering study.[11]

In one Bloom experiment, students in a traditional time-structured classroom produced the standard bell curve of performance, with about 20 percent of the class achieving mastery (earning at least the equivalent of an 85-percent grade), some at the other end of the curve performing poorly, and the rest in the middle. The test group, allowed to self-pace, saw 90 percent of the students achieve mastery. As Rose wrote, "Of course, the conclusion that logically follows from this is both obvious and terrible: by demanding that our students learn at one pace, we are artificially impairing the ability of many to learn and succeed."[12]

Beyond a measure of "seat time"—literally, how long students sit in class and the *assumed* number of hours they study outside of class—the credit hour also functions as a measure of "weight." That is, a three-credit-hour course is assumed to include a certain, if very ill-defined, amount of knowledge covered and grasped by the student. As Laitinen writes, the US Department of Education recognized the limitations of time alone as a measure of learning and issued a 2010 guidance document that said, "At its most basic, a credit hour is a proxy measure of a quantity of student learning."[13]

Nowhere is this idea of *quantity of student learning* vis-à-vis *time* well defined. Experienced academics within a field can look at a course syllabus and generally agree if the topic coverage, depth, and rigor *feel* right for a three-credit-hour course. Curriculum review processes depend on the integrity of faculty and the rigor of review to ensure that a reasonable amount of learning is offered in a course and commensurate with the credit hours assigned. But by taking advantage of this poorly defined standard, unscrupulous education providers, often in the for-profit college sector, have collected substantial tuition revenue based on an excess of credits for too little learning, getting more for less and inflating their profits while decreasing their expenditures. In the end, few would dispute that the credit hour remains a poor and ill-defined measure of weight. Its use as a measure of seat time remains its chief application.

Even in that use—measuring how much actual time a student spends on a course—the credit hour is flawed at best. Institutions must define their use of the credit hour as part of the accreditation process, as required by the federal government.[14] The standard typically is one hour of class time plus two hours of homework time, multiplied by three times per week for fifteen weeks. So, in a typical course, students attend class three hours each week and complete six additional hours of homework. However, only the three hours of class time are *observable and measured*, while two-thirds of this critical standard is unmeasured and wildly variable.

Research suggests that students do considerably less than the formula requires.[15] Students with limited resources who work while enrolled tend to do only what is required and not what is needed. And the standard suffers from a one-size-fits-all approach that fails to recognize that some students will need much less time than two hours of study outside of class, while others will need more, and yet others are unengaged and spend only enough time on a course to squeak by with a passing grade. Students tend to skip large lecture courses in particular—often more than half the classes—and simply get lecture notes from peers. And the rapid growth of online education has mostly been in asynchronous courses, meaning that students are never online at the same time (thus providing the flexibility that busy adult learners need), removing even the one piece of the credit-hour standard that can be measured: time in class with the instructor (though online learning platforms at least record the time a student spends on the platform itself).

A higher education system that is built around a flawed, time-based measure of learning, where class time is the only element we can accurately measure, creates many ripple effects. For example, the system struggles to recognize and account for all the other ways students learn outside of standard three-credit-hour courses. We know students come to us with knowledge and skills. If they have gained those competencies through courses they took elsewhere, our transfer credit policies are inadequate to capture that learning, ultimately disadvantaging those students and wasting money, as illustrated earlier. And while colleges generally offer some credit for learning while students are in high school, through dual enrollment and AP courses, those traditional-path options are not helpful for adult, nontraditional learners.

Yet even less efficient are our ways of recognizing learning that happens *outside* of academic courses and programs, often called prior learning assessment (PLA). Someone who has served as an officer in the military, leading a logistics unit with a great deal of formal training, has a body of college-level knowledge and skills. Someone who has worked ten years as a bookkeeper in the family business, managing contracts, banking arrangements, and payroll, has college-level knowledge and skills. Someone who joined a company with an entry-level job and worked her way up to an executive-level role has a lot of college-level knowledge and skills. Yet we generally do not have good ways of validating that knowledge and those skills and awarding college credit for them.

The American Council on Education (ACE), higher education's primary trade group, has long offered a credit recognition service (used with the military to recognize some of its training, for example), which produces an ACE transcript. But accepting this validation of learning and awarding credits for it remain the prerogative of colleges and universities. The Council for Adult and Experiential Learning (CAEL) has also been a pioneer in prior learning assessment work. The CAEL approach typically feels slow to students, however, who have no way to predict how many credits they will receive should they complete the process, and who face the same uncertainty regarding whether the receiving institution will even recognize those credits. These systems generally tend to function as out-of-touch analog processes inadequate for our digital world.

Examples abound of students receiving far fewer credits through prior-learning assessment than they might have expected.[16] A ten-year veteran of the US Marine Corps might have more than twenty prior-learning credits on an ACE transcript—halfway to an associate degree—but find that she receives only two credits from the college she enrolls in after leaving the military, and that those credits are for physical education, which don't count toward her major. As a 2020 report from CAEL noted, colleges often award large amounts of military credits that count only toward elective courses, rather than toward students' majors or degree programs. In addition, corporations spend billions of dollars on internal education programs, much of it extremely well done, rigorously assessed, and at the college level, but struggle to have this learning recognized within our credit-hour system. PLA also suffers the aforementioned disincentive for universities and their faculty (who often have a final say on the awarding of credits) to accept transfer credits, since every PLA credit accepted toward graduation means less tuition revenue collected by the institution and one less enrollment in a faculty member's course.

While much work is needed to improve prior learning assessment, the practice could help the more than thirty million unemployed Americans reskill, upskill, and get back to work, ACE and the Western Interstate Commission for Higher Education said in a 2021 report:

> In many ways, recognition of learning across the workplace and formal post-secondary education is coming of age, yet again, as it did just after World War II and in the 1980s during the transition from the industrial to knowledge economy. We face a similar time in 2020 of great economic and social uncertainty. We must leverage all the learning available to us with a particular emphasis at the intersection of work and education. ACE believes that the recognition of prior learning can be a catalyst to speed American's human capital toward greater national competitiveness, economic opportunity, and social mobility.[17]

While the credit hour has come to largely define the workings of higher education, it has proved wholly inadequate for what matters most: educating students. The credit hour

- measures student time in class, but not actual student learning
- relies on the help of grades, which get assigned at an arbitrary point in time unrelated to students' capacity to learn, suffer from rampant inflation, are often based on poor assessment practices, and are not trusted by employers or even other colleges

- provides little help in recognizing or assessing learning in all the places it happens outside of the classroom
- remains largely irrelevant to the workforce, where employers care about what students can do with what they know, not how long they sat in class

The credit hour is what we have been stuck with for decades, and it helps us with the weight question—how *big* an associate or bachelor's degree is—but it is woefully inadequate. And interestingly, the activity the credit hour measures with some accuracy, the time a student should have sat in a classroom, is increasingly understood as a less effective way to learn than alternative learning practices.

The COVID-19 pandemic and the sudden shift by colleges to fully remote learning revealed that many students, particularly younger or traditional-age ones, benefit from the structured accountability of a class schedule and time in the same room with an instructor. Students who need that external motivation to complete work often struggle with asynchronous delivery models for remote learning, turning off their cameras, getting distracted, and ignoring emails from instructors. Yet even for traditional-age students who need class time, the research on high-impact learning practices rarely points to the classroom as a powerful venue for learning, instead citing learning activities such as internships, project-based learning, study abroad, and other nonclassroom learning. The time someone sits in class, what the credit hour best measures, is just not that important or useful.

WHAT WE MEASURE INSTEAD OF STUDENT LEARNING

Our education system's reliance on time as a foundation creates even more insidious problems. Because it is so poor at reflecting the quality of actual learning for any given student, the outcomes of education, we have a whole industry largely built on inputs. If we were focused on outcomes, we would say with great certainty what graduates of a given program know, what they can do with that knowledge, what kinds of jobs they typically get and what they typically earn, and how much completing the program usually costs them. Outcomes might also include graduation rates, the gains made by specific underserved student populations (such as increases in income), and the other positive benefits of program completion (for example, the level of civic engagement and good health practices that research cites for college graduates). Those metrics are all outcomes but not one of them speaks to how a program was created and delivered, because that matters little.

However, what we mostly do instead is assess institutions on their observable attributes and what we can measure as an *input*. So, we often cite

- the size of the institution's endowment, or financial holdings
- the percentage of faculty with PhDs
- the ratio of faculty to students
- the amount of research produced and the money that comes in to support that research
- the level of athletics played and the winning records of the teams
- the beauty and amenities of the campus
- college rankings of various kinds

We even used to count how many books were in the library and rank institutions that way, before the digital age.

Because students themselves are an input, we also look to the grade-point averages and standardized test scores of the incoming class, even though those say more about wealth and socioeconomic class than intelligence or capacity. Also, because we associate scarcity with quality, we look at acceptance and yield rates (how many applicants are accepted and then decide to attend) as markers of quality. None of those measures, alone or in the aggregate, tell us anything useful about the quality of learning at an institution or its outputs, with one possible exception. Student GPAs and test scores that are good enough to gain admission into a highly selective college signal to employers that graduates had some level of high academic preparation, diligence, drive, and work ethic *before* college, and that they are likely to bring those qualities to the workplace *after* college. In that sense, much of the value of a Harvard or Princeton University degree accrues with the acceptance letter.

The systemwide effect of inputs and status as proxies for quality and actual student learning has resulted in perverse incentives and skewed priorities across higher education. These include

- an inordinate focus on intercollegiate athletics and obscene spending on stadiums, facilities, and coaches' salaries, while critical campus needs go unmet
- an arms race around facilities, including signature buildings by famous architects and near palatial amenities for nonacademic uses
- a dramatic shift from need-based financial aid to so called merit aid, which seeks to attract better students by giving them aid they do not need in order to attend, and the use of leveraging, which is giving just enough extra aid (often in the guise of an academic scholarship) to make high tuition rates palatable
- the most experienced faculty teaching fewer courses and fewer students, with more emphasis on research and scholarship (and reward and recognition structures that put little emphasis on educating learners)
- growth in specialized accreditations that drive up credentialing demands and serve faculty more than students through mandated class caps and requirements around nonteaching functions like research
- enormous growth in doctoral programs that is disproportionate to actual job-market needs in many areas (especially the humanities)
- obsession with published rankings (and cases of colleges gaming their numbers to get a better spot)
- an inordinate reliance on fundraising, and lack of discipline around cost control and good business practices

Mission creep and spending on the wrong things (usually not on students) tend to accompany institutions' quest for more status in higher education's hierarchy. As Clayton Christensen and Henry Eyring argued in *The Innovative University*, Harvard is held up as the gold standard for quality in the industry, with all other institutions compared in descending order, thus driving the chase for status.[18]

Steven Brint wrote in a recent essay, "When I surveyed presidents of 300 colleges about which institution they would like theirs to resemble in 10 years' time, those who responded consistently indicated that they wanted to move up in the hierarchy—those in the public sector by adding more degree programs and greater research intensity, and those in the private sector by becoming more selective while expanding the size of their entering classes at least a little."[19] The drive for status has become existential for much of higher education, as institutions fiercely compete for students to offset an increasingly failed business model.

The price of that competition is shockingly high, with the increasing national cost of providing higher education doubling that of health care since 1980. The impact on families has been profound, especially as states have divested from higher education and shifted more of the cost of college to students. The total US student debt has ballooned to $1.7 trillion, more than all credit card debt combined, and second only to home mortgages as the biggest source of debt for Americans. While that often-quoted debt number invites some unpacking—a fair bit of it includes unfettered borrowing for graduate education, for example—there is no question that costs have shifted to students and their families. According to a recent article in the *New York Times* on one struggling public university in Pennsylvania:

> *In a nutshell, the burden for supporting the system shifted sharply— from the state to the student. In the 1980s, the state paid 75 percent of a student's load. Now the student pays nearly 75 percent. In Pennsylvania, the average student debt taken on by graduates of state schools rose 35 percent between 2011 and 2018.*[20]

As expected, the high cost of college has had a disproportionate impact on those who need it most and has exacerbated societal inequities based on class and race.

Roughly half of Black students (49 percent) who borrow to attend college will default on their student loans within twelve years, according to federal data that only became available in recent years.[21] The overall twelve-year default rate is 29 percent. It is 36 percent for Latinos, the nation's fastest-growing demographic. This rate is not only unsustainable, but ethically and morally unacceptable.

Meanwhile, higher education is grappling with an increasingly firm national conviction that the system is rigged against lower-income and first-generation college students. Widely cited data on social mobility show that the 38 most selective US colleges and universities enroll more students from the top 1 percent of the income scale than from the bottom 60 percent.[22] Add to that the blitz of news coverage on the Varsity Blues admissions scandal, where hedge-fund managers and celebrities fraudulently bought their kids' admission into top universities, and it's easy to see why just one-third of Americans think higher education is fine the way it is.

Beyond the growing disconnect between who can gain admission and pay for college versus those who cannot, which is most Americans, the gap is also expanding between what the industry offers and what people want from it.

Todd Rose's think tank, Populace, issued a report in 2020 titled *American Priorities for Higher Education*.[23] It explored people's personal preferences for higher education (which are often at odds with popularly perceived opinion, a gap that Populace explores across many areas of public interest). The major findings include

- *The single greatest consideration is affordability.* "Tuition is affordable" is the most important personal and perceived societal higher education priority. However, people underestimate the intensity of that priority for most other people.
- *Glaring differences exist between personal and perceived societal priorities.* When it comes to students' motivations in deciding which college to attend, most people believe that students care about competitive sports, being perceived as elite, an active social scene, and a young student body. Students actually rank those factors among the least important.
- *The public prioritizes access over increased selectivity.* Rather than see higher education institutions develop their own criteria for admission—be it diversity-based or testing-based—Americans want higher

education institutions to develop standard open-enrollment practices, meaning that anyone with a high school diploma or GED can
gain admission.

- *A preference for flexibility challenges the standard four-year
  degree.* "Students are able to choose non-degree pathways" registered
  in respondents' top quartile of priorities.
- *There is a strong appetite for applied learning over academic instruction.* On-the-job training such as internships, hands-on workshops,
  and lab-based classes, as well as instruction from instructors with
  practical experience, all appear in the top ten personal priorities for
  the American public, the college-bound and enrolled, their parents,
  college graduates, and those without a four-year degree.

Americans' preferred higher education system is far from the one we
have today. Not only is it increasingly out of financial reach for far too
many people, undercutting its fundamental role in driving social mobility, but it does not provide the flexibility that is now needed in a world
where people need to learn and retool on a regular basis, as technology
increasingly and more rapidly drives change in the workforce. The system
values status over access, amenities over learning, knowledge over skills,
while 45 percent of those who start a degree program fail to complete and
leave within six years.

Remember Marian, whose story began this chapter? She was in grave
danger of slipping into that 45 percent—risking potentially devastating
student debt that could not easily be discharged in bankruptcy—as she
tried to succeed in a time-based system that was not built for her. Then she
found SNHU's College for America (CFA) degree program, offered through
Duet, our partner organization in Boston. (We often partner with organizations like Duet to deliver our programs in low-income communities.)
Created with the support of the Bill & Melinda Gates Foundation, CFA is a
self-paced competency-based education program built around the mastery
of competencies, not time. Students progress through the program at their
own speed, mastering 60 competencies for an associate degree and 120 for
a bachelor's degree, with assessment conducted through the completion

of real-world projects for which there are no grades—just "mastery" or "not yet." Students face no penalty for resubmitting projects, reflecting our belief that the best learning often occurs in the struggle to master something.

After enrolling in the program and being freed from the tyranny of a class schedule, Marian made rapid progress. When her daughter had a relapse, she simply paused her study and resumed when her daughter recovered. As she said to me, "*I am the calendar.*" It turns out Marian was really smart and really determined—something that was not at all apparent in her transcripts from traditional college programs. She raced to complete her associate degree and is working on her bachelor's, all at a low, flat tuition rate she can afford. Marian will graduate with a degree, with demonstrable skills valued by employers, and the ability to land a good job. She will have substantially improved her daughter's life and her own. Students like Marian, who received career support from Duet while enrolled at College for America, start with an average annual income of $13,999. But they are earning an average of $40,779 after they complete their degree. And 63 percent of Duet participants who earned a bachelor's degree from CFA were either enrolled in a master's program in 2021 or earning at least $40,000 a year. That may not sound like a lot of money. But for these students and the underserved communities in which they live, it is life changing, and the start of a career pathway to better salaries and better lives. Some even move directly into graduate programs. In 2020 we sent our first student to Harvard Business School, an almost unthinkable outcome for him prior to discovering our program.

A NEW HIGHER EDUCATION ECOSYSTEM

Americans long viewed higher education as the foundation for social mobility and opportunity, offsetting societal inequity. It was part of the solution, but now is increasingly and accurately seen as part of the problem. Our higher education system has burdened Americans with student debt levels that are increasing at unsustainable rates, it fails nearly half of those who enroll in college, it routinely produces graduates who are not ready for the workforce or for jobs that go unfilled, and it is increasingly too expensive for families, at a time when nearly 40 percent of Americans report that they would struggle to come up with just $400 for an unexpected expense.[24]

Steven Brint in his essay poses the question, "Is this higher education's golden age?" No. But it could be. Perhaps we need this crisis in higher education and a pandemic to break free from the anchor of tradition and "we've always done it this way" thinking, often reified by regulators. We have the seeds of reform available to us, as constraint and crisis often spawn innovation and creativity. Scalable solutions exist, as we will share in chapter 4, and are within our grasp.

A healthy learning *ecosystem* is, I believe, the answer to a new era of American higher education for what many people call our Fourth Industrial Revolution. In the natural world, healthy ecosystems are replete with diversity and variety, with all parts playing an integral role and supporting each other. This coherence and compatibility are what is missing in higher education. We (myself included) often use the phrase "the American system of higher education," but there really is no discrete system. In contrast, European countries have systems, because higher education usually started with state-sponsored institutions, whereas our higher education industry began with private institutions. Harvard was already two hundred years old when the Land Grant Act passed and kickstarted our public university system. Every country in Europe has its own real and discrete system of higher education, yet the European Higher Education Area (EHEA) helps students navigate the waters of studying in different European countries and ensures that all European systems are interconnected and accessible (even if quality still varies greatly). If a place as diverse as Europe can make it simple to move between different countries, why can't we do the same between our own institutions?

To borrow from E. O. Wilson, the renowned conservation biologist, "insular biogeography" is the idea that isolated ecological areas, being disconnected from each other, are inherently less robust and supportive of life than healthy ecosystems. Our institutions of higher education largely exist as islands and thus are not serving students who try to navigate their educational journey in a world that promises and rewards mobility.

A higher education ecosystem starts with nomenclature, definition, and taxonomy. A well-designed one would have agreed-upon terms and definitions to describe institutional types, programs, credentials, and outcomes. This information would exist in a common and easy-to-understand classification scheme, a modern and up-to-date version of the Carnegie Classification of Institutions of Higher Education, a framework created in 1970 for categorizing US colleges and universities.[25]

The ecosystem would also need data interoperability so that systems and institutions could "talk" to each other. This capability would allow much easier and more transparent reporting, student mobility, and consumer protection. It would readily recognize and accommodate a wider array of providers, forms of learning, and credentials, which means it would need some form of "exchange rate" to make sense of those ways of learning. Healthy ecosystems are diverse (think of the phrase *biodiversity* here), so a learning ecosystem would be designed to encourage and support the diversity and variety we celebrate in American higher education, perhaps our greatest strength. It would create a kind of operating system upon which providers—colleges and new types of education providers— would be like applications, or apps: widely varied, performing different functions in different ways, true to themselves, but all compliant with the underlying operating system.

In this scenario, learning and assessment can go from being "owned" in one place to being distributed across the ecosystem. It means becoming less rigid about what we view as learning and who we view as qualified to educate and evaluate "our" students. It means partnering with the workforce and accommodating both elevated ideas of learning, the liberal arts ideal, as well as the needs of employers and graduates' desires to have more meaningful careers. This is especially necessary at a time when, as the World Economic Forum estimates, 65 percent of students entering college today will ultimately be working in jobs that do not currently exist. In addition, the looming impact of artificial intelligence and automation on the workforce and the speed at which jobs are now changing means that people will be moving in and out of the learning ecosystem across their careers and lives. Sometimes that might be for "just-in-time" learning, reflected in a badge or microcredential, and sometimes it may be for a full-fledged degree. While colleges, universities, and conventional degrees will likely remain dominant within this new ecosystem, we will need to embrace new providers and new types of credentials.

Most importantly, this ecosystem needs to be built around students, not institutions. In many ways, our current approach to higher education has the institution "owning" the student. Financial aid policy and institutional practice make it nearly impossible for a student to self-curate a learning pathway across multiple institutions. Transferring from one college to another can be difficult (in fact, some colleges would not accept into their first-year class the *graduates* of other institutions) and often costly and inefficient. The college major is essentially a one-size-fits-all learning pathway that typically reflects the traditions and structures of a given discipline and the academic department within an institution, rather than what a student might want or need. And institutions own the student transcript, charging to access transcripts even though students earned and paid for their learning.

We often talk about "fit" in finding the right college for the right student. But in the status quo, fit is more about a student conforming to the college than the reverse. That may be necessary if we think about individual institutions as the central unit of concern within an ecosystem. They can only be what they can be—we can't ask a fern to be an oak tree in a forest. However, if we think about students navigating a larger learning ecosystem as our primary concern, we are free to think about their interactions with institutions more fluidly and in a more integrated way. This shift will be vital to changing our shared understanding of the purpose of higher education.

ACCEPTING A COMMON CURRENCY

At a root level, if we are to retain a healthy variety of postsecondary institutions and build out a student-centered learning ecosystem to accommodate more kinds of providers, not just the incumbent set of formally recognized colleges and universities, as well as a greater range and granularity of credentials, we need an exchange rate—a framework that brings coherence while supporting a wide diversity of institutional type, culture, and mission. The deeply flawed credit hour is not that framework. But competencies could be the common currency.

Competency-based education is certainly not a new concept. Its roots go back to the 1860s, when more modern agricultural practices and machinery were being introduced. The Morrill Land-Grant Acts "provided the basis for an applied education oriented to the needs of farm and townspeople who could not attend the more exclusive and prestigious universities and colleges of the eastern United States." Land-grant colleges emerged in rural areas and were more focused on job training and real-life scenarios than theory. Competency equated to things that really mattered to students, like crop yield. And in addition to being more relevant to jobs and careers, these new colleges integrated thinking about how to ensure that students graduated with tangible competencies into their instruction and assessment.

Even so, higher education has essentially been a faith-based initiative for the last six hundred years. Faith-based because people *believed* if a college had enough volumes in its library, enough PhDs among the faculty, and enough students with high standardized test scores, what came out the other end was going to be just fine. What happens when we reverse that? What if we are clear about the claims we make about student learning and how we can back up those claims? These are the two fundamental questions at the heart of competency-based education:

- What claims do you make for your students in terms of what they will know and be able to do upon graduation?
- How do you know?

Being able to answer those two questions with great clarity opens a world of possibilities. These may seem like relatively straightforward queries. But unpacking them reveals a thicket of complexity. It requires asking education providers to be crystal clear about the claims they make for the learning they provide: their outcomes. And providers would need to be rock solid about their assessment of student learning: *how* they know.

But if a newly realized system can do that, we could largely disregard how students achieved their learning. We can be creative, get our hands dirty, make learning more fun and meaningful, encourage new methodologies, capture more forms of learning, and better serve a wider range of students. All of that will enrich the ecosystem. And a healthier ecosystem would have benefits far beyond higher education and college graduates, with more economic, civic, and human thriving.

When we think about competency, the focus shifts from what students know to what they can *do* with what they know, giving students valued workforce skills and helping them demonstrate what they may already know or have learned. That latter point is key. Many students come to higher education with a massive wealth of experience—be it from life, work, the military, or prior education—that sits untapped and untested. Think of a thirtysomething who has hit a glass ceiling after a decade working at a bank. Despite gaining valuable skills and knowledge, she is ineligible for a promotion to a managerial role because she lacks a required bachelor's degree. So, she decides to go back to college to finish a degree program but isn't able to put any of her experience into practice because it's just not part of the assessed learning. *Waste* is the only word to describe that scenario.

A competency-based system would give students credit for what they can do with what they already know. It would let them skip having to retake unnecessary courses to relearn content, which would save them precious time and money. Competencies are more granular, practical, and aligned with what's happening in the workplace. At the same time, they can ensure an understanding of the knowledge frameworks in which skills exist, since skills will often become out of date and reskilling will happen at a faster pace than ever before. Seat-time is no longer the dominant metric of learning, and the traditional credit hour becomes obsolete in favor of assessing actual ability.

Importantly, the ideal competency-based model doesn't place prescriptions or limitations on how students get to that mastery of skills. And it doesn't set time limits. It makes allowances for the unique circumstances of so many students, meaning anyone might complete a course in as little or as much time as they need to master the competencies. Letting students own their learning experience gives them enormous power, motivation, and a sense of pride when they meet their goals. That type of learning experience is scalable, everywhere from high schools to refugee camps. And it's good for employers.

Students in SNHU's competency-based degree programs have to master 120 competencies to complete their bachelor's degree. Each competency is well defined by its component parts. Mastery of a competency requires students to successfully complete each of the parts that add up to a competency. They do so by completing projects—assessments that more closely mimic how that competency will be used in the real world (something our students love for its relevancy). Students set their own schedules and go as fast or as slow as they need, so the program fits their busy lives, not a rigid institutional schedule. All for a fraction of the cost of our regular tuition for traditional campus-based programs.

Annmarie Conway, a College for America graduate, was one of seven Massachusetts Department of Transportation and Massachusetts Bay Transportation Authority employees who graduated from the program in 2018. As a full-time working mother, she was only able to do so because the program was self-paced, available 24/7, project-based, and entirely online. Her employer, upon seeing the results of the program, described the program as a strategy for employee retention.

Jasmine Zamora-Montero, a mother of three and a full-time health-care employee in Texas, was able to complete both an associate and a bachelor's degree in one year through her company's partnership with SNHU, by using the self-paced learning the program afforded. In her unique case, that pace was blisteringly fast. The degree helped her qualify for a supervisor position at her company. These were real, tangible results. Jasmine's experience is also becoming more common as a growing number of employers are expanding tuition benefits to help more of their employees advance—a smart move for companies seeking to retain talented workers.

The benefits of competency-based education extend beyond workplace skills. Our graduates may move through their education in a very different way than their peers in traditional programs, but they have the same liberal arts core. Take this reflection from Sharon Lougee, a CFA graduate:

> *While in the program, I learned about so many things. I learned about Lean Principles, the Federal Reserve, globalization, and the moral philosophies of Immanuel Kant and John Stewart Mill. I learned about the Renaissance, the Reformation, and the Enlightenment while exploring art from masters such as Giotto, Donatello, Rembrandt, Manet, and Picasso. I studied how the earth cycles water, carbon, nitrogen, and phosphorous; the enormity of the Great Pacific Garbage Patch; and the devastating impact pollution is having on sea turtles, birds, fish, and the overall health of our precious oceans. Through CFA, I strengthened my listening skills, practiced giving and receiving feedback, and improved my ability to resolve conflict while working on teams. I even learned how to better manage stress, which helped me juggle work and family while earning my degree.*

This is the kind of statement that would make the president of the most traditional liberal arts college smile.

NO COMPETENCY WITHOUT ASSESSMENT

For a very long time, a college degree was a signal to the labor market that the graduate knew things, could be relied upon to be an able communicator, would have reasonable quantitative skills, and would demonstrate an adequate work ethic. That signal is no longer reliable for many employers, who routinely hire college graduates who don't write well, who don't demonstrate critical thinking skills, and who struggle to do basic math. Colleges often make claims for their graduates—albeit ill-defined claims from a competency-based perspective—but do not apply strong enough assessment practices to ensure their graduates know and can do what they claim.

During a sabbatical in 2015, I worked as a senior policy advisor to Ted Mitchell, the undersecretary of education at the US Department of Education during the Obama administration. My focus was competency-based education and new non-college providers of postsecondary education.

We commissioned the American Institutes for Research (AIR) to do a study of assessment in American higher education. The resulting report was far from positive. Aside from those places where our lives depend on it, such as health care or aviation, reliance on individual faculty grading lacks the rigor (in terms of validity, reliability, and more) that good assessment demands. We like our pilots to have good grades, but we make them take Federal Aviation Administration exams, do time in simulators, spend countless hours in the right-hand seat under the watchful eye of a senior pilot, and undergo periodic retraining. The same is true of nurses, who may get good grades in their nursing program, but still do hours of clinical work, take their board exams, and must satisfy ongoing education requirements. For too much of higher education, we simply rely on run-of-the-mill assessment practices and let rampant grade inflation allow ill-equipped graduates to enter the labor market.

In a new ecosystem, we must be much smarter about assessing the knowledge and skills in any discipline, as well as assessing things that historically have been hard to measure, such as motivation, determination, and critical thinking.

The 2017 Valid Assessment of Learning in Undergraduate Education report from the Association of American Colleges and Universities, a well-respected membership group representing the liberal arts and general education across much of higher education, gave a glimpse into the learning that was happening on US campuses.[26] It found that students could adequately explain issues and provide evidence but fell short on drawing conclusions or understanding the greater importance of issues. They could perform well enough in quantitative areas of math but were less skilled in articulating the "why" and "when" of using it. Likewise, the Gates Foundation–convened Commission on the Value of Postsecondary Education is seeking to define and value the economic returns of education after high school.

The status quo also fails in its assessments of crucial "soft" skills, which Scott Pulsipher, president of Western Governors University, better calls "power skills" or "enduring skills." How do you measure something like trustworthiness or grit without being invasive, offensive, or judgmental? This requires good assessment in which we identify the behaviors we see in trustworthiness, then put students in situations where they must exercise those qualities, and assess their performance against a rubric or list of criteria for demonstrated success. Simply measuring the low-hanging fruit of knowledge isn't working for anyone and certainly isn't giving us a full picture of the real ability and potential of students. When today's graduates get to the workplace, often they are baffled by the expectations of their employer. That's a two-way street, as employers often are baffled by how little their new hires can do. While graduates may be confused or out of their depth in the workplace, they may simultaneously be limited in understanding their own ability and potential because no one has drawn it out of them, or even tried.

In his book *Out of Our Minds: The Power of Being Creative*, Ken Robinson makes the case that students often leave schooling—the big chunk of their youth spent in the classroom—with very little understanding of their own creative power or ability.[27]

If competencies are our currency, assessment is the gold standard to which it is pegged. We must get the assessment piece right because it is at the very heart of the model, and well-designed competencies without rigorous assessment are just as flawed as the credit hour. Instead, the system needs to meaningfully measure the right knowledge, skills, and abilities, which must be tethered to real life. Robinson writes,

> *I asked a professor of nanotechnology what they use to measure the unthinkable small distances of nanospace? He said it was the nanometre. This didn't help very much. A nanometre is a billionth of a metre. I understood the idea but couldn't visualise what it meant. I said, "What is it roughly?" He thought for a moment and said "A nanometre is roughly the distance that a man's beard grows in one second."*

Defining *nanometer* is a display of knowledge. But translating a memorized term into a practical example displays genuine mastery of the concept. We should strive to register that kind of mastery in our own assessments, making learning more relevant to students. Our competencies are only as good as our assessments. And only by doing assessment right can we have the highest-quality programs that produce the most successful graduates.

How will we know assessments are working? They will connect to the workforce and give students the meaningful knowledge and related skills that translate to better opportunities and social mobility. If you accept the idea that robust assessment can prove competency in an area, you ought to care less about how students get there. Once you accept that assessments can prove competency, you then accept into the ecosystem *any* provider—a traditional college or not—that can demonstrate efficacy. Suddenly education becomes very exciting and so much more like the memories we all have of our most impactful learning experiences. Game-based learning, learning during travel, on-the-job projects, you name it. We can disrupt delivery models and be free to try anything that shows itself to work. The common currency of the competency-based credential will work at any type of institution in the ecosystem. No institution that is doing good work with its students—and can demonstrate it—should be threatened by competencies.

Many will be threatened, of course. Moving such a large, established industry to a new foundational standard will be profoundly hard. Jobs will change. Status will shift. Institutions will cede some control to the student. And as with all change, moving to the use of competencies as currency will result in winners and losers among colleges. In an ideal world, higher education would move toward collective, agreed-upon definitions of competencies and shared assessments, though that is an especially heavy lift in an industry that so fiercely guards institutional and faculty autonomy.

While a growing body of evidence shows that competency-based education can work better for many students, the going has been slow. Most forays by colleges have been limited experiments. Even so, 57 institutions were offering at least one competency-based program in 2018, according to a survey by AIR and Eduventures.[28] And 430 institutions reported being either interested in giving it a try or in the process of creating a program. Importantly, some colleges and universities have proved that scale is possible. Western Governors University, which has one of the nation's largest student enrollments, is entirely competency-based. Capella University has also been successful with the delivery method. More than eight thousand students had graduated from its competency-based FlexPath program by 2019.[29]

Innovations in higher education tend to follow a predictable course. Figure 1.1 from Gartner, a technology research firm, is a useful tool for interpreting developments in education technology. Take massively open online courses, or MOOCs. Nine years ago, many predicted that the free, online courses from MOOC providers would take a big bite out of traditional higher education, with the *New York Times* declaring 2012 "The Year of the MOOC."

The fall from the "peak of inflated expectations" was brutal, however.[30] MOOCs quickly became the butt of jokes in the industry as the

FIGURE 1.1

Visibility/Time Matrix: Plateau of Productivity

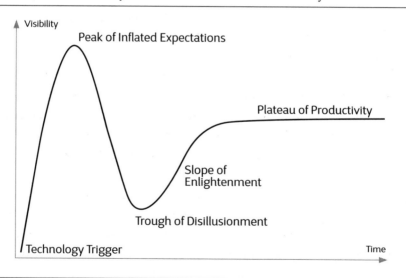

big providers scrambled to find viable business models. But while many observers disregarded these online course companies during the "trough of disillusionment," Coursera and edX have quietly retooled and grown to be serious players in higher education, building scores of fruitful partnerships with universities and employers. And their role in disrupting the market for online graduate credentials may just be starting.

There is so much magic in the constellation of our higher education system, but it is fragmented and confused. When it comes to cost, we are like passengers on airlines, all paying different rates for different flights. Some of those flights go somewhere, some involve long layovers and multiple legs, and some of them go nowhere at all, regardless of price. If we get this right and develop an ecosystem that offers value for everyone, we can then organize and bring meaning to our existing institutions and see the proliferation of new types of learning for all types of people. We can also make college affordable again. A student in SNHU's online program who starts out with no previously earned credits can earn a bachelor's degree for just $40,000, less than one year's tuition at many private colleges and less than the total cost of a degree at many public institutions. Western Governors University offers its competency degree program for just $6,000 per year. In College for America's "all you can consume for one price" competency-based degree option, Zach Sherman, its first graduate, raced to an associate degree in under one year for a tuition price less than $3,000.

Rethinking our higher education system requires us to make sense of what we have while ensuring that we're all speaking the same language. It's about giving people a fair shot at being rewarded for what they've learned, what they know, and what they can do with what they know. Giving people education and credentials that are meaningful and real will go a long way toward diminishing the existential threat higher education is facing. It's also about building a system of higher education genuinely designed for a new era. Our current disjointed system was built for and informed by a nineteenth- and twentieth-century industrial model. It has become calcified, with a regulatory framework that is too often glacially slow to change, and because of a culture of institutional self-centeredness and complacency. The higher education ecosystem we need will put students at the center. It will be interoperable and fluid. It will unlock opportunity and upward social mobility for millions of additional Americans through a system that everyone understands, that is transparent about itself and its performance, that innovates with accountability, and that performs exponentially better than the status quo.

CHAPTER TWO

COMPETENCIES, NOT CREDIT HOURS

LET'S BEGIN WITH A THOUGHT EXPERIMENT. Imagine we are forming a new society and that we are members of a team tasked with inventing the higher education system. We have been given the end goal of creating a system that prepares people to do the work they need to thrive, to be thoughtful contributing members of our community, and to have intellectually enriched lives. A tall order. Because good design works *backward* from goals, we go to the next question: "What will we measure to know we were successful?"

Our team brainstorms, and we write three options on the whiteboard.

- *Knowledge:* Decide what students should know and then assess them on that knowledge.
- *Competency:* Decide what skills or competencies they should demonstrate and assess their level of proficiency in each.
- *Time:* Decide how long it should take to learn on average and base student progress on time.

35

Considerable debate ensues. Knowledge proponents argue it is hard to do anything without knowledge, which should be the foundation of our new higher education system. If we know what someone knows, we can reliably *infer* what they can do with that knowledge, they say.

The competency proponents readily concede that knowledge is important and a prerequisite but argue the real measure of our system's success will be in student performance. Knowing about something is not good enough. Our new society needs to have confidence our graduates can *do* what we need them to do within their chosen fields.

The group that proposes time as a measure of learning points out that we have a scale challenge with a lot of people to educate and we need to standardize in a way that moves people along in an efficient manner. They also say performance is often time-bound—think deadlines or emergency situations—and that time also can offer a way to measure an *amount* of learning.

We know all three options have value. For example, our community members need knowledge about how our government works to be good citizens. The engineers who build our infrastructure will need some knowledge of mathematics and physics. Citizens will be better able to appreciate art museums if they know something about art. Lawyers and judges need detailed knowledge of the law and an understanding of its spirit and intent before working on a single case. Educators must have some understanding of child development and our theory of education before we put them in an elementary school classroom.

Knowledge proponents finish by saying, "If we do a really good job with knowing, we can trust that our graduates will be able to do the work of society, to contribute to their communities, and to have enriched lives." They want to spend the rest of the time talking about *content*, what knowledge we need to include in the curriculum.

While competency supporters agree that knowledge is a key foundational element in meeting our three goals, they argue that the real test of learning is what students can *do* with what they know. They think efficacy is best measured in actual, not inferred, performance. It's great that a new doctor can explain the biology and chemistry and physics involved in stemming blood flow when someone has a deep cut. But can they treat the wound and heal the patient—acts of *doing*? They appreciate the ability of a graduate to describe the importance of a free press in a healthy society but want evidence that graduates can discern reliable journalism from propaganda and understand what constitutes evidence to support an interpretation. The competency proponents admit that art and literature have intrinsic value for the delight they bring but believe greater value lies in the capacities they build: the literacies that give people better command over language, the ways of knowing and thus thinking, and the ways of recognizing beauty and deriving pleasure from it. These capacities are tools, they say, and tools are for using.

Competency proponents conclude by saying, "If we can measure our graduates' proficiency at doing what we deem important, we can infer the knowledge required to get them there and know if we have met our goals." They spend the rest of the time talking about *assessment* of performance and how students can demonstrate what they can do with what they know.

During the debate, the group working on a time option tapes charts up on the wall to rationalize the education system. They have decided how long each phase of schooling should be as well as roughly what age students should be during those phases. They construct a calendar for the school year and how much of which subjects should be covered. They map assessments onto those time frames. They show how budgets can be built, how staffing can be allocated, how much space is needed, and how to provide financial support for the students who need it. Some argue that using time allows us to see who is smarter, because those students will race ahead and perform better on exams than their less-capable peers. They argue that we were asked to build a system that everyone can understand, and they dismiss questions about what students should know and be able to do, trusting faculty and institutions to sort that out at the local level.

They finish by arguing, "If we build a system that everybody understands, we can leave those academic arguments about knowledge and skills to the local institutions." The group spends the rest of their time talking about *time*, what constitutes satisfactory progress for a learner, how much content should be included in a learning period, and when we give up on a student.

The knowledge and time supporters form an alliance. Those in the former group have a passion for their subject—sometimes taking up the mantra of "knowledge for knowledge's sake"—and have no real quarrel with mapping what they want to teach onto a preordained time frame. In fact, time provides a useful measure of *weight*, or how much knowledge can be covered over what amount of time. They also like the way time emphasizes coverage (did I cover all the content by the end of the term?) over performance (can my students do what I was supposed to ensure?). The emphasis on coverage shifts the burden of efficacy to the students, allowing the system to determine who is good, mediocre, or poor by fixing assessment to a specific moment in time, the final exam or paper.

The competency team is outnumbered and largely loses the argument, winning support for only one position: to measure performance for disciplines that are responsible for health and safety. Everybody agrees they want pilots who can land and take off, and surgeons who can make and close incisions. Those areas will feature non-time-based performance assessments, such as additional exams, clinical work, simulators, and expert sign-off on performance checks. In fields where lives depend on both learning and doing, time will not be fixed. Learning, demonstrated through more rigorous exams and performance-based assessments, will be nonnegotiable and fixed, while time will only be established as a minimum.

An aspiring pilot with a perfect 4.0 GPA in a college program still will need to pass rigorous exams from the Federal Aviation Administration, log a set threshold of flying hours for each level of licensure, and fly under the watchful eye of more experienced pilots and instructors long before being allowed to move from the right-hand seat in the cockpit of an airplane to the left-hand seat of a captain. The pilot will also need to periodically demonstrate through recertification tests that her skills and health have not eroded. Same with medical professionals. Great grades in college and medical school are expected. But board exams also are required, as is a minimum of clinical hours completed under the watchful eye of an experienced professional, before an aspiring nurse or doctor is deemed ready to treat patients. You can be an accountant by simply completing courses in an accounting degree program, but you must take very rigorous exams (and usually must complete a lot more study) to become a certified public accountant (CPA). Even here, performance-based assessments hold onto aspects of time (using competencies as well as the minimum numbers of hours required, a belt-and-suspenders desire for reassurance, I suppose).

In our thought experiment, time is the answer to the question, "What will we measure to know we were successful?" The knowledge advocates can live with the system. Competency proponents take solace in the fact that where education matters most, where rigor and assessment of performance are critical, they have carried the day. We build our postsecondary system and base it on time. Knowledge is unitized in periods of time, relying on something we call the credit hour. The credits add up to become courses, which are offered over fixed periods of time we call terms or semesters. Take enough credit hours by taking enough courses over time and you earn a degree, assuming you do not fail courses along the way.

We understand that students graduate with wildly divergent levels of actual knowledge. And we largely agree to not talk about how poor our assessment practices are in most fields (again, except for those areas where we need our graduates to be very capable performers). In lieu of strong assessment, the agencies we create to ensure our colleges and universities are of high quality instead measure various attributes or inputs they associate with quality. They look at the faculty who will be teaching, the facilities in which that teaching will occur, the level of access to the knowledge sources students will need, the processes the institutions have in place for creating curricula, and so on. They look to ensure that suitable processes are in place and, increasingly, they look for evidence of performance. The government agency tasked with managing financial aid for students to help pay for tuition embraces the time basis for learning and creates a framework based on time, with rules for how long students can take to complete a course or program as well as time-based measures for satisfactory academic progress. We have built a system of postsecondary education on a foundation of sand moving through an hourglass. It's the one we live with today in the United States.

INNOVATION AND REGULATION

Higher education is a regulated industry. A key reason for this is that most Americans cannot afford to attend college without federal financial aid. So the operations of almost all colleges and universities in the country are regulated by the Higher Education Act of 1965, which periodically gets revisited, revised, and renewed by the US Congress. (The last time was in 2008.) Title IV, one of the law's eight sections, governs the administration of federal financial aid. As a result, this section largely prescribes much of how higher education is structured, and that starts with the credit hour, our time-based measure of learning. However, buried in the bureaucratic regulatory language, in section 34 CFR 668.10(a)(1), are the seeds for an alternative to the credit hour, through something called direct assessment. This is defined as "an instructional program that, in lieu of credit hours or clock hours as a measure of student learning, utilizes direct assessment of student learning, or recognizes the direct assessment of student learning by others."

In a subsequent subsection, the law says:

Direct assessment of student learning means a measure by the institution of what a student knows and can do in terms of the body of knowledge making up the educational program. These measures provide evidence that a student has command of a specific subject, content area, or skill or that the student demonstrates a specific quality such as creativity, analysis, or synthesis associated with the subject matter of the program. Examples of direct measures include projects, papers, examinations, presentations, performances, and portfolios.

This obscure section of the Higher Education Act first came to my attention in 2012, during a small professional gathering in Miami organized by Educational Testing Service (ETS), which administers the SAT, GRE, and other standardized tests. At that meeting, Amy Laitinen, who had worked at the US Department of Education and the Obama White House and would later write *Cracking the Credit Hour*, mentioned the direct assessment provision in Title IV. She said no institution had yet used direct assessment, which she said could offer an interesting alternative to time-based measures of learning.

I was intrigued. By then SNHU had become one of the fastest-growing universities in the country, driven by enormous expansion of our online programs. *Fast Company* had ranked the university number twelve in its "World's 50 Most Innovative Companies" list, and we were growing so fast that we were onboarding between thirty and forty new full-time staff members every week.[1] We primarily served working adults who needed to complete a degree to create better opportunities for themselves. Most had tried college before and had not finished, sometimes because life got in the way, or because of finances, or because they simply had not been ready academically. Fully 80 percent of our undergraduates held credits they had earned previously from more than one institution. Most worked full time, had families to care for, and were now going to squeeze in an education. We often said they were driven by the Four Cs:

- *Credential:* They needed a degree to unlock access to a better-paying job or career path.
- *Convenience:* They needed their program to work in the context of busy, over-scheduled lives with too little time.
- *Completion:* Most of our students felt stuck and were facing work and financial pressures, so they had a sense of urgency. They wanted a path to completion that could get them a degree as quickly as possible.
- *Cost:* They needed a college education at a price they could afford.

Because SNHU has always focused on first-generation college students, working-class families, and students for whom a college degree might be most transformative, we were determined to reduce the cost of a degree.

That determination was reinforced by the still severe impacts of the Great Recession. Many people were unemployed or struggling in its aftermath. It would take ten years to get back to pre-recession employment levels. So many of our students faced a precarious situation. With little social or financial capital, they were one unexpected car repair, unpaid doctor's bill, or change in work schedule away from dropping out. I was

preoccupied with this twin challenge of cost and time and had been looking more closely at innovative new delivery models.

With members of my team, I visited Western Governors University
in Salt Lake City, the undisputed leader in competency-based education, which, while still tethered to the credit hour, had dramatically low-
ered the cost of a degree. I was also interested in the open courseware
initiative from the Massachusetts Institute of Technology, which offered
high-quality course content for free, and in Carnegie Mellon University's
Open Learning Initiative, with its early use of machine learning for
instruction and assessment.

Long flights can be the best place for me to think big. During a flight
home from Malaysia in 2011, I typed up a "thought paper" for our team
titled "The Next Big Thing." It imagined a flexibly timed, low-cost subscription model of learning that would focus on assessment rather than
how one learned.

The benefits of the model I imagined included that

- We could be more certain about what students have learned when
  they complete courses and programs and earn credits.
- We could make seat time variable and learning fixed, a long-needed
  reversal of our current model.
- Getting into college would be simple and easy, as we wouldn't really
  care what students brought to the table. But getting out of college
  would be hard, and students couldn't leave without demonstrably
  mastering the learning outcomes set out for them.

I also included a challenge: make the program as close to free as possible, knowing that we would have to rethink almost all of our assumptions about what is required to provide a high-quality degree.

DIRECT ASSESSMENT

At the time I couldn't see how we could create this form of competency-
based education, in part because of the rules governing our federal

financial aid system. Then came the lightning-bolt moment at the ETS meeting in Miami. Laitinen described how existing law allowed for a never-attempted new form of competency-based education, one not grounded in the credit hour or measurements of time at all (at least in concept; the truth later proved to be more complicated).

That evening, in the hotel lounge, my SNHU colleagues Yvonne Simon and Martha Rush-Mueller (who had played major roles in the early growth of our online division) and I met with Laitinen and pressed her for details. We had no existing models to consult, no case studies from the Education Department or an accreditor, so we couldn't predict what regulators would require or how they would evaluate any eventually proposed program. But we wanted to create a disruptively innovative model of education that would work better for the students we sought to serve, "to revolutionize higher education," as I had said in my thought paper.

The term *disruptive innovation* had been coined by Clayton Christensen, the famous Harvard Business School professor, a longtime friend, and a member of the SNHU Board of Trustees, in his wildly influential 1997 book, *The Innovator's Dilemma*.[2] Christensen used the term, now broadly discussed and adopted, not to describe "sustaining innovations," which allow one to better compete by the existing rules of a business sector—say by improvements in quality, efficiency, cost, or speed—but by rewriting those rules and disrupting the incumbent industry leaders.

Car companies largely compete on sustaining innovations, such as improvements in performance, new styling, improved reliability, or value. In contrast, Airbnb disrupted the hospitality industry by inventing a new approach to lodging that did not play by the same rules as the hotel industry. One of the lessons of Christensen's research is that while sustaining innovation best happens within the incumbent business, disruptive innovations happen at the margins and are more likely to flourish when the mother ship—the core existing business—is kept at arm's length. I would need a small, separate group to create this new direct assessment program. And part of my job would be to protect this program and insulate it from the rest of SNHU. The reason wasn't that the university was ill-intentioned or not innovative. As Christensen's work showed, disruptive innovation never makes sense within the existing paradigm and the natural organizational dynamic. Like the human body confronting foreign matter, incumbent systems are designed to incorporate or kill off disruptive innovation.

I had learned this lesson. In 2003, when I set out to take our university's nascent online business and grow it, online education was still considered disruptive. The small eighteen-member team of our online division was tucked away at the far end of Stark Hall, a nondescript building on campus. Its operations were enmeshed in the well-established governance and operations functions of the traditional, residential campus. The program served a few hundred students and felt little urgency to grow or do much more. When I first walked through the team's space, most of the staff members were in offices with their doors closed. I saw little discernible energy or even work going on, except for one student advisor in an open cubicle, who described her work and that of her unit with conviction and enthusiasm. She was Amelia Manning, and would years later come to head SNHU's online division, educating tens of thousands of students.

Even by 2003, I knew the nontraditional-aged students we had long served were finding online education to be a better alternative, one that worked for their busy, time-constrained lives. But nonprofit higher education mostly viewed online education as inferior. Into that vacuum stepped the for-profits, led by the University of Phoenix, which grew to enroll more than five hundred thousand students at its peak, in the Great Recession's wake, when the sector was educating 12 percent of all college students.

Those large online providers were disrupting higher education. I wanted to compete with them. And while few would admit it then (or now), major for-profit college chains did many things better. They were more focused on students, even talking about "customer service," a phrase most of nonprofit higher education still won't use. They worked hard to understand adult learners and their needs, were much more data driven in management and decision-making, had the accountability and discipline

Can utilize appropriate tools and techniques for effective collaboration on remote teams.

The competency is further defined through a set of mastery statements:

- *Can coordinate the creation of project timelines and meetings for a distributed team.*
- *Can use tools and technologies to effectively collaborate with remote team members.*
- *Can communicate effectively in a distributed team environment.*

Students are then given instructions for three projects they need to complete as part of a hypothetical situation in which they lead a remote team's ability to work well together (being able to lead teams is a high-priority skill for employers). In the first of the projects, students must demonstrate these two skills:

- *Can coordinate the creation of project timelines and meetings for a distributed team.*
- *Can use tools and technologies to effectively collaborate with remote team members.*

We tell students this:

In Project 1, you will set up a project in project management software, which will mean creating the project, project tasks, and project timelines and meetings. You will also create a conference call invitation using the template provided. In Projects 2 and 3, you will work with your team members to improve their remote communication.

Students get directions, links to relevant materials, and then see the rubric we use to assess their performance (see table 2.1). While the competency must be mastered overall, the rubrics allow for more definition, precision, and transparency regarding what is required for success (by comparison, students in traditional courses often get grades with little understanding of what those grades are based on). Students

TABLE 2.1

Sample Rubric for a Competency on
Working with Distributed Teams

Rubric criteria	Mastered	Not yet
Creates task assignments and task due dates for a distributed team		
Creates a visual representation of a project timeline for a distributed team		
Schedules a meeting for a distributed team that clearly outlines agenda items and accommodates individuals in different time zones		
Utilizes project management software to create task assignments for team members		
Utilizes project management software to create project timelines		
Utilizes conference call technology to schedule a conference call and create a link to access the conference call using an online conference call service		
Written answers are clear; use correct grammar, sentence structure, and spelling; and show an understanding of audience and purpose		
Lists sources where applicable using citation methods with no major errors		

in competency-based programs never have to guess at what success looks like.

Students must achieve mastery for each item in the rubric. There is no sliding by with mastering 70 percent—or even 90 percent. Getting a "not yet" communicates success yet to come to the students, rather than failure. And they aren't penalized for addressing the shortcoming. Students simply work to improve that area and resubmit when they're ready. If students can demonstrate mastery quickly, that's great. Time to move on to the next competency. If they take multiple tries, so be it. Remember, in a competency-based education model, time is *variable*, learning is nonnegotiable.

We debated the rigidity of our "all items must be mastered" stance. Some argued that mastering 90 percent or 80 percent on the rubric should be good enough. We could identify some items that must be mastered, they said, rather than requiring them all. I suspect this is a more reasonable, fairer proposition. Should we hold students in competency-based programs to a higher standard than their peers in credit-hour-based courses? Yet if we say learning is fixed, we mean learning is fixed. I don't want my pilots to be good at everything but the landings, or my surgeons to be excellent at everything but identifying internal organs. That said, in many areas we get more competent with repetition. And while a student might demonstrate mastery in writing, for example, subsequent projects within a program will require more writing, a form of "spiraling," to borrow a term from K–12, which builds mastery over time and through levels of increasing proficiency. While a student might demonstrate mastery in basic writing competency, it will still be included in future rubrics in the curriculum, as in the preceding example, further reinforcing the skill and allowing us to stand behind the claim of mastery.

Inevitably, proponents of competency-based education run into the criticism that the performance of skills is all well and good, say in writing or doing math, but that large swaths of college-level learning do not lend themselves to competency-based claims. That is simply untrue. It betrays a bias (or perhaps a kind of intellectual snobbery that also looks like intellectual laziness) based in a tired "knowledge for knowledge's sake" unwillingness to declare what students will learn and be able to do with their knowledge.

Competencies can be assessed across virtually all academic disciplines. Take philosophy and ethics, for example. As I described in a 2014 monograph:

> *To illustrate, one area of study for the associate in general studies degree requires that students examine ethical perspectives. In this area, students explore a variety of essential ethical questions—whether torture is ever justified, for example, or whether people should be able to sell their own organs. In another area of study, students consider the environment by examining the environmental impacts of common products—like bottled drinking water—and show whether they can both calculate the specific carbon footprint of the industry and generate solutions to mitigate it. Students must show they can identify and analyze ethical issues raised by scientific and technologic developments*

by analyzing the infamous Johns Hopkins Lead Paint Study (in which researchers put children in potentially dangerous living situations) and determining whether or not it violated ethical principles of science. They engage in questions about globalization and the meaning of "corporate responsibility." They look at advertisements and examine the ethical issues involved, such as in marketing to children.

They also read important thinkers on the questions under consideration. For example, in the torture example, students read Michael Sandel's 2005 lecture "What's the Right Thing to Do?" and Sam Harris's "In Defense of Torture," and they study Mills on utilitarianism and Kant on duty-based ethics. Their work is assessed against a well-defined rubric that asks them to spot issues, apply relevant philosophies, provide evidence for their analysis, and identify ethical flaws in the argument. In these examples, students engage very explicitly with the kinds of thinking, analysis, and application of ethics that support civic learning. In CFA, there is greater clarity of claims about and confidence in the actual learning (and the ability to demonstrate both) than most institutions possess. And because these elements of civic learning are explicitly built into the curriculum, they become crucial to it. Students cannot graduate without completing these competencies, and they are not the tangential add-ons one sees in many institutional efforts.[3]

The humanities and liberal arts teach many competencies that employers covet, more so now than ever. Top consulting firms recruit philosophy majors because that rigorous discipline makes people competent in critical thinking, reasoning, logic and symbol systems, the nuance of language, and much more. These are immensely valuable skills. But tell a friend that your son or daughter is majoring in philosophy and wait for the inevitable joke about where they will be flipping burgers after graduation. Even President Obama (the professor president!) made a gentle jibe about the humanities in 2014. "I promise you, folks can make a lot more, potentially, with skilled manufacturing or the trades than they might with an art history degree."[4]

Obama quickly and thoughtfully apologized for his off-the-cuff remark.[5] But the widespread attitude of dismissiveness toward the liberal arts, and a decades-long decline in enrollments in the associated majors—art history, philosophy, English, history, and others—is at odds with the growing need for the very competencies those fields develop in students. As workplace skills and technology change at a rapidly accelerating pace, the competencies associated with the liberal arts will be necessary for graduates who will constantly relearn, reskill, and adjust during their careers. Particularly in demand are competencies in communication, navigating difference, learning to learn, and problem-solving, all of which are necessary for ethics, participating in a functioning democracy and civic life, and other areas beyond the job market.

Employers want both those competencies that make a college graduate useful on their first day of work as well as those developed by majors that are often derided in our public discourse. And calling this latter category "soft skills" is ironic, as they are much harder to teach, develop, and assess than so-called hard skills like coding and math. This is a big reason why so many graduates in the humanities eventually enjoy higher earnings than their peers in more technical fields. STEM majors lose their wage advantage steadily, as technical skills become obsolete and they face increased competition from younger graduates. For example, research has shown that by age forty, graduates of social science and history programs typically have closed the wage gap or even surpassed the earnings of computer science or engineering graduates.[6]

The more important point here is that competency-based education can work for any field of study, not simply the vocational ones. Moreover, if academics in fields that have long been in decline owned the competencies they develop in their students, rather than spurning them, they might see a resurgence in enrollments and more public support. And if disciplinary guardians were willing to go a step further by including some of the immediately useful competencies employers most want, their graduates would do well not just over time, but have more opportunities immediately after graduation.

As a study from Burning Glass Technologies notes, by simply adding account management skills (ones associated with sales) to an English degree, graduates from Florida Atlantic University more than doubled expected earnings in their first year in the workforce.[7] Parents might worry about their child deciding to major in music at the prestigious Berklee College of Music. Yet the LinkedIn profiles of Berklee grads show that Google and Apple are among their top employers. The champions of liberal arts education should not resist competency-based education; they should embrace it.

Creating and mapping competencies for humanities major is more challenging. But they tend to age better once completed. Use improves them. The more one writes, the better one gets at it. And these competencies are typically foundational, relative to their STEM counterparts, and thus evolve more slowly. In contrast, keeping competencies up to date in technical fields is a real challenge, as the technologies evolve rapidly and often quite dramatically.

The president of a well-respected engineering school, a colleague and friend, worries that the slow pace of curricular development and the governance processes associated with this work are making her graduates less well prepared for careers than they should be. She wants her faculty to move faster to keep up with industry, while integrating more of those enduring skills that will help graduates be better learners long after they graduate. Fields that have great rigor around assessment—often requiring additional assessment and special licensure—recognize this challenge and usually require continued education after graduation. For example, continuing medical education (CME) and continuing legal education (CLE) require annual updates in many states. Because competency-based education programs are much clearer about the claims they make for their students than traditional credit-hour-based programs—with their reliance on time and unreliable assessment practices—it is easier to see whether a program is, in fact, current. That transparency is a strength of competency-based education and puts pressure on educators to stay relevant and up to date in ways rarely accomplished in traditional programs.

It is commonplace to hear college graduates say they learned more about their field in the first six months of their new careers than they did in four years of college. I remember taking journalism courses in college and then landing a job at a small-town paper in Massachusetts, the *Palmer Journal*, and covering everything from town meetings to car accidents to high school football, as well as writing ad copy and obituaries on the side. I too felt that I was learning so much more in the *doing* of journalism than in my actual courses. However, like most students who feel this way, I was too dismissive of the newly acquired knowledge I was able to bring to my work from my college studies. My traditional education focused on the knowledge of journalism, but not the skills required to put that knowledge to work.

One of the central strengths of competency-based education is that it unites knowing and doing. Our students routinely praise the relevancy of their projects and describe the ways they earn mastery one day and put those competencies to work the very next day in their jobs. Their employers take notice, in large part because they think in terms of competencies, in terms of what their people can do well and what they need to do better. Competency-based education gives higher education and employers a shared language and framework, one that has long been missing in much of higher education.

Shifting to this model does not necessarily require faculty to change their instructional approach, their pedagogy. In fact, with its focus on the end result or output of mastery, competency-based education is agnostic about *how* a student gets to that level. As a result, it invites more innovation around delivery, which encourages new ways of learning and approaches that bring down the cost of education. (We'll see four case studies that do both in chapter 4.) Nor does the model prescribe *what* claims a program makes for its graduates.

American higher education became the envy of the world in part because of its great variety of institutions. This constellation of providers, including new ones, can continue to differentiate themselves in whatever manner they see fit and as their missions allow. Rather than dictating the claims an institution makes, competency-based education requires only that they be transparent, shifting the assessment spotlight from knowledge alone to demonstrable competencies and the knowledge that supports them.

In 2015, I led the design of Educational Quality through Innovative Partnerships (EQUIP), an experimental program for the US Department of Education, which, among other things, sought to support the development of more competency-based education programs. In the Federal Register notice announcing the program, we included this language:

1. *What measurable claims is the institution making about the learning outcomes of students participating in the program? For example:*
   - *What is the evidence that the learning claims are commensurate with postsecondary- or post-baccalaureate-level work?*
   - *Do the institution's statements about student outcomes capture requisite knowledge and skills? How?*
2. *How are the value and relevance of those claims established? For example, what external stakeholders have been consulted to verify the value and relevance of the claims?*
3. *How will the claims be measured?*
4. *How will institutions be held accountable for meeting those claims?*
5. *How do all the claims for learning come together into a meaningful and coherent set of overall program outcomes and goals?*[8]

The significant items here include accountability, the value and relevance of the learning, and the inclusion of measurable skills alongside knowledge. How an institution and its faculty deliver on those is entirely up to them.

Dismantling the hidebound, time-based status quo won't be easy. Despite the pedagogical freedom a competency-based system offers to professors and instructors, change is hard. Many will resist giving up the lecture-heavy, seat-time-focused form of learning. And tearing up administrative systems that colleges have long relied on is sure to provoke resistance. But both faculty members and administrators will quickly see the benefits of competency-based learning, most importantly for their students. Just as the massive shift to online learning in the spring of 2020, prompted by the pandemic, has prompted many faculty to look anew at their teaching and to better appreciate the complexity of building well-designed learning experiences.

Likewise, creating meaningful, high-quality competencies is a laborious process. As it should be. Designing a better framework and currency for college-level learning than our time-based status quo is obviously a crucial step in ensuring that students get value out of their credential. And the work that goes into the creation of a competency raises an important question: does something like this happen for traditional, credit-hour learning? (*Answer: No, it doesn't.*) Making the shift to competencies would mean, for many faculty, surrendering the wide license they have in creating course titles and descriptions in course catalogs (after that, what they do is pretty much up to them), instead working in the sort of collective fashion that is necessary when everyone has to agree on the more fine-grained delineation of competencies.

The process at College for America features a ten-step curriculum design process. After crafting and refining the initial program description and outcomes definitions, the academic subject matter experts who lead this work hold the first of three reviews with stakeholders, including representatives from relevant industries. They build out the competencies around a mutually agreed upon understanding of future work in the discipline, receiving feedback from a wide range of university stakeholders. At each step along the way, the program's designers further hone competencies and the program pathway, with final workshops and a formal review before the curriculum is submitted for approval under the university's governance structure.

The product development phase is just as involved. Faculty members design and refine course content and projects, ones designed around authentic work scenarios. They build out that content, curating learning resources and creating formative assessments that are designed to support the projects. Subject matter experts and academic leads review and approve the projects and resources. Eventually the content is edited, multimedia designed, and the user experience built. All these components are then tested in the learning management system.

The competency is never truly finished. Even after final revisions and the program's launch, any worthwhile competency must be revisited continuously for improvements. The academic leads gather feedback from learners, student advisors, faculty members, and employers—both through individual feedback as well as more formal surveys. That intel is incorporated into the ongoing quality revisions to the competency, making it stronger over time.

With the proliferation of competency-based programs over the last five years, the field has gained an understanding of what is required to develop high-quality programing. The Competency-Based Education Network (C-BEN), the leading organization in the field, offers a *Quality Framework for CBE Programs* and has provided quality assurance reviews for over twenty institutions. In addition, the C-BEN–led Competency-Based Assessment Collaboratory is a group of institutions working to identify hallmark practices in assessment, the cornerstone of high-quality competency-based education.

MICROCREDENTIALS AND SKILLS-BASED HIRING

The advantages of a competency-based education model extend well beyond greater clarity about what students can do with what they know, the invitation to innovate around teaching methods, and the possibility of designing new, lower-cost delivery models. While a college degree was once a signal to the labor market that a graduate possessed basic skills upon which an employer could build—say communication skills, quantitative reasoning, critical thinking, and even deportment—that signal is today widely distrusted. This distrust has contributed to a yawning disconnect between higher education and the workforce, though community colleges are generally better on this front than their four-year college brethren. Employers worry that college graduates are coming to them without foundational skills or those needed in technical and emerging areas. Even in the middle of the last recession, millions of jobs went unfilled.

Most employers still use the college degree as a proxy for job seekers' skills and knowledge. Yet a growing number of large companies, particularly in information technology, are dropping degree requirements in hiring. IBM has been among the most aggressive, saying it prioritizes the right mix of skills over traditional degrees for 15 to 20 percent of the company's hires each year. IBM says these "new-collar" jobs are in the fast-growing fields of cybersecurity, cloud-computing, cognitive business, and digital design.[9] The company, which employs 360,000 workers, points to the wide skills gap in these fields, noting that colleges and universities produce roughly 70,000 graduates with computer science degrees each year, about one-tenth of the supply needed for open tech jobs in the US.

"We have more jobs than we have people to fill them," Kelli Jordan, IBM's director of career and skills, said in 2019.[10] "So we really started to think about how we could bring more candidates into our pipeline, how we could open up the aperture of skilled resources so that we could actually meet our hiring goals."

Other companies have followed suit, including Google, Penguin Random House, Whole Foods, Hilton, and Apple.[11] The federal government also has pushed for more of a focus on skills over degrees in hiring for its huge workforce.[12] Meanwhile, the Society for Human Resource Management (SHRM) has offered support, publishing guidelines for how to adopt skills-based hiring practices.[13] Advantages of this approach include bigger, better talent pools. Equity gets a boost as well with less of a reliance on degrees as a proxy for knowledge and skills and what SHRM calls "pedigree-based hiring," in exchange for more objective ways of gauging a job seeker's aptitude.

The shift toward skills-based hiring forces employers to think harder about the competencies needed for a job. That, in turn, can strengthen the bond between higher education and the workforce. Employers and colleges both benefit from working together to define needed skills, ones HR offices can prioritize in hiring. Clearly defined competencies coupled with rigorous assessments that employers can actually trust (unlike grades on transcripts, which they do not trust) allow employers to hire graduates confidently from any college or university. And all institutions can rise to the challenge of showing what their graduates can do. For example, when software engineers from California's Foothills Community College demonstrate talent and skills that equal those of graduates from Stanford University (and there is little reason to think that they cannot), the elite technology companies can stop using university brands as a proxy for skills in their hiring processes and cast a wider and more equitable net in their relentless search for talent.

College credentials are more relevant in the workforce when employers can better trust the knowledge and skills that graduates possess. And jobs are easier to fill with a more diverse pool of potential hires, who are also more likely to succeed. Most importantly, a competency-based education system helps students avoid racking up risky debt on the flimsy promise of a well-paying job on the other side of a graduation they may not see.

Competency-based education and skills-based hiring also better support the learning that today's college graduates will need to engage in over the length of their careers. During the industrial age, one might have attended college for four years, graduated and begun work, and never set foot on a campus again. Today's graduates, however, will be engaged in constant reskilling and upskilling, dipping in and out of our higher education ecosystem for various lengths of time and for a greater array of credentials. That might mean a degree. Alternatively, students could earn a badge or microcredential that represents a set of skills or competences in a small bundle, offered over a shorter time, maybe two months or two weeks or even two days. The fastest-growing segment of higher education is microcredentials and certifications, often college-level work with a focus on some key skill area needed in the workforce.

College degree holders are hardly the only Americans who need new skills. Those without degrees suffered the most in the Great Recession and again in the pandemic. And financial need means that urgency to get into the workforce and start earning money usually trumps the deferred payout of enrolling in a degree program that is likely to take much longer than two or four years to complete. The recently unemployed, according to a national survey by SNHU, want educational options that are fast, inexpensive, and directly tied to job opportunities.[14] That theme was reflected in the previously mentioned *American Priorities for Higher Education* report by Populace, where survey respondents expressed interest in nondegree pathways. Many Americans face desperate circumstances, and competencies, skills, and a job are more important to them than a degree.

Even so, competency-based education models can work well in the creation of degree pathways based on microcredentials that can be stacked together to form a degree, without forcing students to waste money and time to retake courses as they move in and out of college. Higher education experts and policy makers are increasingly focused on this so-called stackability as a crucial fix for the fragmentation and inefficiencies of higher education today (see figure 2.1). If time were no longer the foundation for this system, it is easy to imagine that someone could earn a credential in six months, land a job in a high-demand field, and then over time complete subsequent credentials in a pathway that leads to a degree. That time frame and flexible path would allow far more students to reap the huge benefits of a college degree, which is still the best ticket to the middle class and a rewarding career.

Although a stackable path is theoretically possible with conventional three-credit-hour courses, the microcredential world is focused on competencies and skills. And traditional credit-hour-based courses, with their lack of transparency on competencies, just don't lend themselves very well to this emerging sector of learning. This line of thinking is why SNHU recently acquired Kenzie Academy, a small provider that offers six- and nine-month programs in software engineering and user experience (UX) design, both hot fields. With a focus on underserved populations, Kenzie gives its students a combination of soft skills and measurable tech skills, placing them in jobs with an average annual pay of $57,000.

Because Kenzie offers college-level work, we will now be able to award credits to their graduates, starting them on a path to an eventual degree. (Most of Kenzie's competitors in the coding boot camp space serve students who arrive with degrees in hand; Kenzie's mission is to educate underserved students, many of them students of color.)

Most of traditional higher education has not yet embraced competency-based education and is thus poorly equipped to compete in

FIGURE 2.1
Stackable/Pluggable/Building Blocks/Possible Configurations

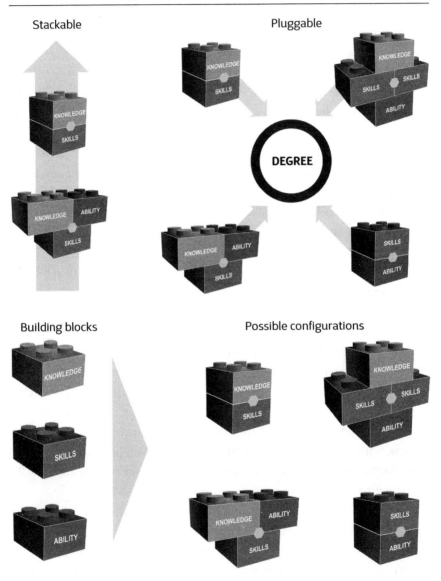

the sub-degree market. As a result, much of the action in this space has been led by Kenzie and other boot camps; MOOC providers like Coursera, edX, and Udacity (though MOOC providers are not doing competency-based education or even rigorous assessment for the most part); and other new providers. To help more low-income Americans access these programs, which can improve their lives much faster than traditional college degree programs, we will need to rethink our federal financial aid system and regulatory frameworks (more on that in chapter 5). This nascent sector of postsecondary learning is messy because it does not yet have a clear taxonomy and nomenclature. But several national efforts have emerged to provide some much-needed clarity.

Credential Engine, for example, is working on a centralized, cloud-based registry of current information on all US credentials, including everything from college degrees to apprenticeships and professional licenses.[15] This nonprofit, which estimates that there are a total of nearly one million unique credentials in the US, is using technology and a common language to create a searchable database of all the credentials it identifies. This is a big job. But even as that project continues, alongside similar work by QA Commons and Workcred to help embed competencies and industry-recognized learning into curricula, we know that measurable competencies rather than credit hours should and will be the foundation of a new learning ecosystem.

Imagine a new normal where students can see what knowledge and skills are required to earn a credential. Where faculty can help students get there any way that works, using their skill as instructors and assessors of knowledge to make verifiable claims about students' abilities. Where employers can hire with confidence and have access to talented hires, including job seekers who lack the advantages of wealthy peers who were able to afford a residential college and relied on the brand stamped on their diploma to help them land a good job.

This vision is no fantasy. As we shall see in chapter 4, viable models are up and running, with groundwork being done now to quickly scale up across the nation. What has been missing is the urgency to create a new framework that would empower that growth. Sadly, by worsening inequity in higher education and further exposing the weaknesses of a time-based model, the pandemic has made crystal clear that it's time to try something new.

CHAPTER THREE

THE HARDEST WORK

Assessment

MY 2015 STINT AT THE US DEPARTMENT OF EDUCATION was focused on what came to be known as the Educational Quality through Innovative Partnerships (EQUIP) project. The idea was to encourage collaboration between traditional colleges and nonaccredited providers, while also trying out alternative forms of quality assurance. We would need to ensure that the student learning in this experiment was verified with solid, authentic assessments. And I thought we would benefit from some outside help to get a better sense of how assessment in higher education was faring.

The American Institutes for Research (AIR) agreed to do a pro-bono primer on the state of assessment and report for the department. What they discovered was even worse than I'd feared. The state of assessment was somewhere between awful and dismal, according to the AIR primer. It didn't pass muster on anything—validity, reliability, you name it. The situation hasn't improved much since then. The consensus these days among learning experts is that assessment in higher education remains a "hot mess."[1]

To be fair, it's understandable that the industry has struggled so much with this crucial piece of higher education. Assessment may be the hardest work, for both traditional college programs and competency-based ones. As we've established, colleges and their accreditors have failed to develop broadly applicable standards for student learning, a shared understanding of learning *outcomes*, essentially what students need to know and be able to do to successfully complete a program or course. The assessment of student learning tends to be left to individual faculty members, who have typically received little or no training on how to get assessment right. Yet given the complexity of assessment and its importance to ensuring academic quality and the value of college credentials to students and employers, it's a mistake to encourage faculty to essentially just wing it when trying to measure student learning. Doing so also squanders an opportunity to make assessment an instrument of learning for students, rather than simply a periodic judgment.

Even assessments that appear demanding, academically rigorous, and on-target with the required learning in a course too often fail psychometric measures of *reliability* and *validity*. Put simply, validity in assessment is the extent to which it measures what it is supposed to measure. Does the test or performance-based project yield measurements of the learning in question, instead of something else? For example, if an assessment mostly measures how fast students can fill in multiple-choice answers on a test, rather than their mastery of learning concepts, it isn't valid. In psychometrics and statistics, reliability is the consistency of the measure. If the assessment produces similar results under similar conditions— students tend to score on a stable grading curve, say, to use the traditional college model—then it has a high level of reliability. Inter-rater reliability means that if you and I were assessing the same student's work, we would come to the same conclusion and assign the same grade or score. An assessment is reliable if its results are precise, reproducible, and consistent when conducted multiple times. But it can be reliable without being valid. A clock that is consistently ten minutes fast does not give a valid read of the time.

To be trustworthy and academically rigorous, assessments must be both valid and reliable. While getting this right is far from easy, it's also eminently doable. Faculty members and program designers can tap a large and growing body of research to inform their work on assessments. Unlike in traditional higher education, where the default too often has been to throw up our hands and rely on inadequate measures of learning—weak assessments and mostly meaningless grades—competency-based education requires good assessment. That's because without it, we can't stand behind our claims about what students know and can do. And clear and transparent claims without commensurately strong assessment practices are not helpful. They invite abuse by unscrupulous providers and undermine trust in the integrity of the learning model.

Paper-and-pencil tests are the age-old standard for measuring learning in higher education. They can be graded quickly, particularly if the assessment is in a simple true/false or multiple-choice format. And instructors often use an electronic grading system to test large numbers of students more easily. They can also rely on these static forms of assessment, whether multiple-choice tests or research papers, in each reiteration of a course. Many faculty members use similar tests for years, maybe making small tweaks from term to term. This approach allows instructors and institutions to compare the performance of different groups of students over different terms, but it does not actually help them gauge what was learned (if not mastered) and what wasn't in order to make changes and improve both the instruction and the assessment for future courses. It is important to note here that using assessment to improve pedagogy begs the question of whether the competencies themselves are right. My computer science program might have excellent assessment practices, but if I'm assessing student mastery of FORTRAN, I've got some bigger issues. In other words, if I get better at teaching and assessing the *wrong* thing, I still have a problem. That said, assessment could be used to inform improvements in the how the course is taught, and to adjust course content and testing to reflect developments in fields of study. But instead, the conventional forms of assessment fail to use meaningful measures of student learning to improve the academic experience.

Anyone who went to college will remember classic "summative" exams, which are designed to evaluate what students have learned. These tests are given at set points in time—milestones throughout the course and at the end. The idea is for the test to compare student learning to a standard, or outcome, that is set by the instructor and, ideally, the relevant academic department of the college. Yet too often assessments are only loosely aligned to the outcomes. And while exams are designed to measure if students can remember, identify, or understand concepts that are related to those outcomes, they are far less likely to provide any information about whether students can apply that knowledge outside of the classroom.

For example, an introductory biology course in ornithology might include as an outcome the goal that students be able to identify wild birds of the northeastern United States. A student might succeed in identifying static images of birds on the test, or in recalling distinctive features of a particular bird. But if the student can't identify the bird when she spots it through her binoculars as it flies overhead, has the student mastered the required course outcome? The assessment in this example is a typical proxy for an intended outcome, but it does not actually address the essence of what we want the student to learn in the course.

Elody tried traditional college twice, attending both a small liberal arts college and a regional public university before eventually enrolling at College for America through Duet. She earned an associate degree there in just five months. Then, while working full time, she earned a bachelor's degree in management in less than three years. Elody says assessment was part of what didn't work for her in college prior to CFA:

During my education, I really felt like I wasn't really learning. I was more memorizing the material and just trying to pass a test rather than being able to apply what I'm learning. And when you're not interested in what you're memorizing, you tend to crash and burn.

Those summative exams, which tried to assess Elody's learning at set points in time, rather than gauging more lasting mastery, also reinforced for her how the traditional course material wasn't taking hold. She didn't have that problem with a competency-based model built on project-based learning. "I was actually applying what I was learning to a certain scenario," she says, citing examples of using a gameshow to illustrate probability or a company's revenue to drive home the effects of globalization. "I can actually retain that information better," she says. And because she was required to master the material—and to prove it through assessment—Elody says her instructors knew she understood every single concept.

FACULTY RESISTANCE

Conventional college assessments and grading are grounded in an intrinsic flaw: faculty members are grading themselves. The reason is that academic departments often use student evaluations of teaching to help make personnel decisions about faculty members, including decisions about tenure, raises, and more. Professors know that students who get good grades are more likely to give them high marks on evaluations. This knowledge creates a perverse incentive for faculty members to be lenient in grading, as research has found, and to structure courses to be entertaining and require little work.[2] It's a tacit deal: *I won't grade you too hard, and in exchange you'll give me reasonable course evaluations. We're all in this together.* That conflict helps explain why the grade inflation of the last couple decades has been accompanied by a decline in the amount of time students spend on their studies. And all this feeds into a general lack of rigor with grades, which in turn has rendered college transcripts virtually useless for employers.

How can a system of higher education that has been firmly established in this country for decades, even centuries, not have developed a better way to determine what students have learned? The science exists.

Researchers have long known how it can and should work. Yet despite having little training in how to do assessment right, many faculty members are hostile to efforts to improve it, particularly the higher up you go in the status-obsessed industry's pecking order.

Molly Worthen, an assistant professor of history at the University of North Carolina, Chapel Hill, captured this sentiment well in a 2018 opinion piece in the *New York Times*.[3] She derided learning assessment as a "bureaucratic behemoth" that "seeks to translate the subtleties of the classroom into PowerPoint slides packed with statistics" and reduces "learning to a list of job-ready skills." She challenged the idea of assessment itself, portraying learning as being nebulous and immeasurable. Worthen was right that much of what currently passes for assessment badly misses the mark. And UNC graduates typically do not suffer in the job market despite the insufficiency of college-level assessment, some would argue to a large extent because of the academic aptitude they brought to their first day at Chapel Hill. Yet meaningful, disciplined assessment works just as well for humanities programs at selective universities as it does for professions where everyone agrees traditional exams and grading aren't enough—doctors, lawyers, engineers, and accountants.

Authentic, performance-based assessments require students to demonstrate genuine skills that are needed on the job. This category is broad and can include short answers or essays that are part of summative exams. But proving mastery through *doing* is at the core of the sort of rigorous, performance-based assessment that is growing in popularity in higher education.

Take an air traffic management course, for example. A student might excel at remembering the regulations around flight patterns, dutifully shading the dots in a multiple-choice final exam. But the Federal Aviation Administration still requires students to pass its air traffic pre-employment test and to have three years of "progressively responsible work experience" before they can receive full certification as an air traffic control specialist.[4] "Because of the serious nature of this work and zero margin for error," the FAA says on its website, "the training regimen and proficiencies needed to become an air traffic control specialist are demanding."

When margins for error are small or nonexistent—like guiding multiple airplanes through crowded skies into O'Hare Airport—our educational systems have figured out how to adequately measure proficiencies and competencies. Why not for the rest of us? Is the best way to assess our learning either multiple-choice tests or PowerPoint lists of job skills? This is a false choice, of course. Performance-based assessment in almost all cases trumps the sort of static testing our system is built on, or the dystopian bureaucracy augured by Worthen. And academics who resist good assessment are selling their disciplines short if we accept that paper-and-pencil tests are not enough to determine whether students know how to do something, that course outcomes ideally should require that students can demonstrate or perform their knowledge, and that the performance of relevant skills and knowledge is a good way to encourage student engagement. We should treat the humanities as being just as worthy of quality measures of learning as we do nursing, law, and other disciplines.

Processes vary widely for developing rigorous, high-quality assessments grounded in performance, offering plenty of leeway to instructors. But the good ones generally include the following steps:

- Identifying the performance outcome, likely starting with an "action" verb such as *create*, *draw*, or *build*.
- Identifying whether the instructor is assessing a process (meaning a dictated set of steps to follow to get to the relevant outcome) or a procedure (multiple pathways to get to that outcome) or a product (possessing the sought-after qualities, as in a painting or musical composition).
- Identifying the extent of the real-life relevance of the assessment, based on viability, safety, and other factors. For example, an aviation flight student may demonstrate the outcome of knowing the processes for safe flight through flying an airplane, but an air traffic control student will need to perform processes for that occupation through simulations because of the relative risks of those activities (crashing a single plane versus causing multiple ones to collide).

- Designing the performance assessment with contextualized elements, such as simulations of performance, actual performance, or real-life work samples, which should be verified for authenticity.

The creation of authentic assessments provides an opportunity for college programs to be better aligned with the needs of employers and to leverage those relationships to get ideas on simulations, role-plays, scenarios, and other approaches to designing assessments. Employers also can serve in mentorship roles with students and provide feedback on student performance. The broken link between higher education and the workforce in the US has been a serious problem for years. By rethinking assessment practices to include employers, colleges can take a big step toward better aligning learning and work. Humanities professors at prestigious universities who argue that being focused on getting a good job is a crass or undeniable trait for students are doing a disservice to both students and their disciplines.

Advances in technology are making performance-based assessments more powerful, engaging, and easier to create. For example, SNHU students who were enrolled in a game and simulation design program created an immersive simulation to train emergency room nurses at the renowned Boston Children's Hospital. Researchers at SNHU Labs, the university's research and development arm, received a $1 million grant from Google to build a game-based environment to assess "soft skills" like teamwork and collaboration. In partnership with the education company Pearson, the Labs team is also using machine learning to develop an automated teaching assistant for writing instructors, one capable of assessing student writing in the style and manner of the faculty member to whom it is "assigned." Likewise, in 2020 Arizona State University launched a new virtual reality immersive biology curriculum in partnership with Dreamscape Immersive, an entertainment and technology company.[5] Anyone who has lost all sense of time playing an engaging computer game, with such startlingly real graphics, can appreciate the power of these environments. And high-quality simulations bring transformative potential when applied to both learning and assessment.

When we make well-designed and authentic assessment part of the learning process, we also counter the epidemic of cheating that has swept across higher education with the pandemic and move to fully remote learning for so many students. Faculty are assigning exams to be taken at home in unsupervised and unprocotored settings, exams that assess the ability to provide the right answer instead of actual learning, and are then upset that students are cheating. I sit on the Board of Directors for Chegg, a learning support company serving more than six million students and often accused as aiding or even incenting student cheating. While it now offers tools to prevent cheating on exams, Chegg can see in the data that those exams are being used again and again without change (sometimes for years), are often taken from publisher test banks, and rarely assess actual student learning. As Ray Schroeder argues:

> *While the students who turn to cheating would seem to be too lazy, busy or unable to learn the assigned material, one can often also say that faculty members may be too lazy, busy or unable to design custom assessments that are relevant, unique and promote creative/critical thinking. The "objective" test is founded in the realities of life prior to the 21st century.*[6]

He goes on to argue for authentic assessments as a way to "vaccinate against cheating." Moreover, in an age of ubiquitous information, free content, and search engines, the idea of simply getting the right answer seems hopelessly outdated when genuine learning and the ability to demonstrate its application should be the standard for students *and* faculty. Get the assessments right, and cheating becomes infinitely harder to do.

THE BIG LIFT

The single best form of assessment is rigorous observation by someone who is an actual expert on the learning and knowledge in question—medical students going on rounds in the hospital with a veteran doctor, for

example. Competency-based education inherently requires the student to
do performance-based assessment. In many ways, this is the big change,
the primary hurdle for the industry in moving toward competencies.

When we created College for America, SNHU's first competency-based
program, we framed every competency in terms of a "can do" statement—
what the student would be able to do upon achieving mastery. And when
we designed CFA's credential tracks, we began with the assessment, tying
it to the competencies we needed to measure. What is the thing that we
want people to do really well? Then, working backward, we unpacked all
the discrete pieces the student would need to understand and master in
order to do that task. Those competencies could then be broken into levels
of mastery. This approach essentially reversed how courses and programs
are designed in much of traditional higher education, where the professor
and department determine what knowledge to convey to students, then
tack on the tests and assignments to try to measure how much students
have learned or mastered. Fields like nursing, engineering, and teacher
education are notable exceptions.

So, it's relatively easy to see how performance as a measure of learning
works well with technical or "hard" skills. But how about the humanities?
Let's take writing, which is commonly cited as a major deficiency in today's
college graduates. In fact, written communications skills topped the list of
attributes employers seek on a job candidate's resume, according to a 2019
survey conducted by the National Association of Colleges and Employers.[7]

What are the attributes of a good writer? The answers to that broad
question are too amorphous. To create competencies and assessments,
our academic design teams drill deeper into the components of knowledge and ability. They ask if the student's writing is mechanically and
syntactically correct, if they can create a sound and convincing written
argument, and if the student has a sense of voice and can choose the right
tone for an audience—say for an essay published by a literary journal
versus a note to a fellow student.

The key here is to back into the learning and to ask: what would a
student need to know to write well? Then we can construct course content

and assessments which treat knowledge as the foundation of learning how to do something, rather than the end goal in itself. Likewise, this approach allows us to make the assessment of that knowledge authentic or rooted in the real world. Learning how to do something in the classroom certainly has value. But can the student perform on the job or elsewhere in their lives? That's where the rubber hits the road. And competencies tend not to be used in isolation. The memo you write at work obviously isn't in itself the point—it's the information conveyed in the memo, which will typically tap several other workplace competencies. In addition, writing and other competencies in the humanities must be taught within disciplines, to verify that learners can apply these skills and knowledge appropriately in different contexts.

Assessing student knowledge through the performance of real-world tasks is a superior approach. And it's particularly well suited to competency-based education. An example of a project from College for America illustrates how this assessment can work. This competency project comes from a bachelor of arts in communications degree, which includes concentrations in health-care management and business. It is used in other competency-based programs at the university and serves as the equivalent of a core general education course under the traditional college model.

Here's a summary of the project scenario we present to students: You work for the Thirsty Beverage Corporation and have been in the same job role since starting at the company three years ago. Your team has swelled to twenty coworkers, up from five, due to Thirsty Beverage's rapid growth.

The team is a diverse group. You work well with some colleagues but have had conflict with others. In addition, the team has had growing pains of late, including these issues:

- Some of the new employees have said that they feel frustrated by the lack of training and clarity in job roles.
- You and the other two original employees are feeling the stress of constantly needing to train the new employees and answer their questions.

- With so many new hires, the company's leadership was not able to create a unified team. Now, the diversity in personalities and backgrounds has caused conflict among the team members.

A management position recently opened up on the team. You have decided to apply, and know two other original team members are also applying for the position. The company's leadership is aware of conflicts on the team. So, as part of the interview process for the new management position, they have asked you to develop a communication plan. Your plan should explain how you will effectively collaborate with your team members and create positive team dynamics. To help you develop your plan, leadership has shared some demographic information about your team. (The student gets this simulated demographic information.)

The project's directions for the communication plan include these required discussion points:

- *Team Dynamics:* Before you can develop a plan to manage yourself and your team, you must first analyze the team dynamics of the specific team. This analysis will then inform the development of your collaboration strategies. As you analyze the team dynamics, be sure to
  - Describe the age and cultural differences among the people on the team.
  - Based on these differences, describe the implicit biases that might be at play on the team. Explain how these biases may impact team communication.
  - Describe difficult situations that may occur with challenging employees on the team. How will these situations make communication more difficult? For example, what might happen when you have to manage your coworkers who were not promoted?

- *Personal Approach:* As part of your communication plan, the hiring committee has asked you to explain how you will manage yourself as a leader. Specifically, how will you use what you know about emotional intelligence to analyze your personal approach to management? How will this knowledge help you manage the specific team dynamics?

As you describe your personal approach, be sure to

- Describe how you will assess your own strengths and weaknesses as a leader and your plan to continuously improve these skills.
- Explain how you will address your own biases and use empathy when communicating with the diverse team.
- Explain how you will manage your emotions when working with challenging team members.

- *Collaboration Strategies:* The hiring committee has also asked you to explain your strategy for collaborating with the team. As you develop your plan, be sure to
  - Explain how you can create a safe, open environment that encourages feedback to build relationships within the team. For example, will you establish specific group norms?
  - Describe how you will take culture and age into consideration. How will you promote effective collaboration within this diverse team? For example, how will you ensure that communication is relevant and appropriate for all members of the team?
  - Describe the strategies you will use to collaborate with challenging employees. For example, how will you manage the employees who did not receive the promotion?

The communication plan must be 750 to 1,500 words long, and students are told to include references, citing their sources. Because transparency is a key part of our approach to performative assessment, we share the project rubric in advance with students. They are told that their project submission must meet the detailed list of specific expectations shown in table 3.1 to demonstrate mastery of the competency. We stress that they may resubmit the project as many times as they need to until they can demonstrate mastery of each row in the rubric shown in the table, essentially subcompetencies for the project.

TABLE 3.1

Sample Rubric for a Competency on Team Dynamics

Team dynamics	
Describes the age and cultural differences among the individuals on the team	☐ Mastered ☐ Not Yet
Describes the implicit biases that might be at play on the team, explaining how these biases may impact communication	☐ Mastered ☐ Not Yet
Describes what kinds of difficult situations could occur with challenging employees, discussing how this might affect team communication	☐ Mastered ☐ Not Yet
Personal approach	
Describes the approach to assess strengths and weaknesses as a leader and a plan to continuously improve these skills	☐ Mastered ☐ Not Yet
Explains how to address biases and use empathy when communicating with the diverse team	☐ Mastered ☐ Not Yet
Explains how to manage emotions when working with challenging team members	☐ Mastered ☐ Not Yet
Collaboration strategies	
Explains how to create a safe, open environment that encourages feedback to build relationships within the team	☐ Mastered ☐ Not Yet
Describes how age and cultural factors will be considered to help the team work together effectively	☐ Mastered ☐ Not Yet
Creates strategies for collaborating with challenging employees	☐ Mastered ☐ Not Yet
General	
Clearly conveys meaning with correct grammar, sentence structure, and spelling; shows understanding of audience and purpose	☐ Mastered ☐ Not Yet
Lists sources where needed using citation methods with no major errors	☐ Mastered ☐ Not Yet

An important note here is that this assessment builds on a student's previously mastered competencies, such as collaboration, management of diverse teams, and conflict management. This project allows the learner to get more practice in the use of those recently acquired competencies. In turn, many of the subsequent competencies in the program include writing components, which are assessed to ensure that the student has mastered and maintained competency in writing.

FLEXIBILITY AND REAL-LIFE APPLICATIONS

Seeing the relevance of this exercise to students' lives is easy. And the rubric is designed to allow for the sort of faculty oversight you would see in assessment for pilots and nurses and other life-and-death jobs—rigorous assessment by an expert in the field. Students can use the competencies they have learned, and proved they have learned, right away in their jobs. This immediate payoff gives a boost to student engagement and reinforces the value of their work toward earning a degree.

But communications is one thing, a skeptic might say. What about a liberal arts degree, which is harder to break into discrete learning objectives? We've already shown that philosophy is a bad example of any purported misalignment between the humanities and competency-based learning—as the big consulting firms know, the skills embedded in a quality philosophy program can most definitely be viewed as competencies. So, let's talk about theology. Our skeptic might grudgingly admit that a philosophy major's understanding of the logic needed to parse Kant's take on metaphysics is well suited to competency-based education. But can the theological training of a minister at seminary really be broken down into competencies?

Definitely. And don't take it from me. The Sioux Falls Seminary has helped lead an ambitious competency-based reboot for the field. Greg Henson, president of Sioux Falls Seminary, says his initial interest in what he and his peers now are calling competency-based theological education (CBTE) grew out of their worries about a "growing, deepening chasm between the academy and the field," specifically churches, nonprofit organizations, and social work providers. Even as student loan debt levels in theological education have risen rapidly, outpacing the rate of increases in other disciplines, Henson says that student outcomes have been headed in the wrong direction for theology, with growing numbers of graduates not finding the right fit at a church or another employer. And he says the problem is about academic philosophy. "We tended to assess quality in terms of consistent processes. But what happened, though, is you had a

lot of people who went through those consistent processes and the outcomes were vastly different."

In essence, assessments in theology were neither valid nor reliable.
There was too much variability in the interpretations of student performance by different faculty members. Students were told that if they
successfully went through the academic pathway, they'd arrive at a certain point on the other side—succeeding as a minister at a church, for
example. But that just wasn't happening often enough, Henson says, with
churches citing an array of problems with graduates, including that they
weren't good enough leaders, preachers, or business managers, among
other complaints. "That's why the chasm started. Because you started
having churches say, 'Hey, this just isn't working.' And what we tended
to do in the academy, at least in my experience, was to say, 'We'll just fix
that by making better courses or by making better pathways.'" But that
approach to fixing the problem won't work, he says, because assessments
in conventional programs tend to be too limited. They fail to account for
the wide array of contexts in which theological students use their knowledge and skills after graduation. Henson explains:

> We were developing degree programs as if we were creating a gradu-
> ate to serve in a context. But the reality is, standards of excellence are
> contextually defined. We have a student who is a missionary in Saudi
> Arabia. Leadership as a non-white, non-Western missionary in Saudi
> Arabia is very different than leadership as a nonprofit leader in rural
> South Dakota. But they both did a leadership degree, and we enforced
> one pathway on them. You're going to fail one of the two of them. And
> what we ended up seeming to do—and I say seeming because it's not
> true all of the time—is not serving either one of them because we were
> imposing a context or imposing one definition, which then impacted the
> outcomes. It's impossible to build a structured, required pathway that
> allows for the contextual definitions of mastery. You cannot do that.

As a result, Henson says he began to focus more on the outcomes than
the pathway, to reverse engineer curricula, course material, and assessments with the goal for students—the outcome—as the starting point of

their academic journey. That's what led him to competency-based education, which offers more freedom from time as well as more flexibility around the context of learning and knowledge. In the competency-based seminary program, a student doesn't graduate until all the program outcomes are true for them. And using those outcomes as markers of progress is the way to get to the end goal.

"If you double down on the outcome, then the pathway to that outcome can be infinitely flexible," Henson says. "It's more like an artwork that's collaboratively developed with the student and, in our case, the mentor team, versus a directional path."

In 2014, Sioux Falls Seminary launched Kairos, its competency-based program, which offers master's and doctoral degrees. The online program now enrolls roughly a thousand students in thirty different countries, with focuses in seventy different denominations. The enrollment has doubled during the pandemic. And debt levels for Kairos graduates are far lower than is typical in theology. This approach also gives a boost to equity, by helping to ensure that learning and assessment are contextualized by geography. The defining characteristic of the program, Henson says, is that the competencies focus on academic content, character, and craft. Throughout their time in the program, each student works with the same three-person mentor team, which includes an academic, a vocational, and a personal mentor. The instruction and assessments draw from the relationship between students and their mentors, and the mentor team assesses all the outcomes. The process begins with the student working with their mentors to develop competencies within their context, working off the standardized outcomes—what the seminary calls "contextualized discipleship and customized mastery." It's a postmodern approach, based in an appreciation that the mastery of Biblical acts of Jesus looks different for a pastor in rural southern Brazil than it does for a minister in Atlanta.

Assessments are structured like the committee defense a doctoral student must go through for a dissertation. That's the case for every outcome at every program level. And the assessment could be an oral defense or a capstone project. "It's going to end with the student and the mentor team, as a group, walking through mastery of content, character, and craft relative to that outcome," says Henson. "You either have it, or you don't." Students also do self-assessments for each outcome three times—at the beginning of the program, at the end of each outcome, and when they complete the program. And mentors use data from those self-assessments as learning tools for students.

The mentor teams observe their students throughout the program and get to know them on a personal level. As a result, Henson says, assessment feedback comes with a power that is different than in traditional college programs. Because students have a relationship with their faculty mentor, and have built up trust in that relationship, they can better hear the assessment feedback than they would in a conventional program, where the faculty member's authority is more role-based. This is particularly true with difficult feedback. For example, a mentor might tell a student that she must learn to be humble and teachable, which is the sort of frank guidance that is difficult to give in a classroom and even harder for students to embrace. To move in this direction requires letting go, Henson says. He explains:

> We need to distribute power. The academy has held onto power for a long time, and we need to let go of some of it. We need to distribute the power of assessment and distribute the power of program development, because the academy is not the keeper of pedagogical truth.

The Association of Theological Schools, which accredits 270 graduate schools of theology in the US and Canada, has been supportive of innovation by the Sioux Falls Seminary and other early pioneers of competency-based theological education. The association's board has adopted guidelines for schools that are looking to take the plunge, including a requirement for a coherent plan for assessing competencies, based on clear rubrics and benchmarks, with an expectation that students master all competencies before any degree is awarded.[8] Steven R. Graham, senior director of programs and services for the association, says the results from competency-based theological education indicate it is a very effective model. That may not be surprising, he says, because theological education traditionally was about competencies. Graham praises

competency-based theological education for helping the discipline redis-
cover its root models of contextual training and assessment, such as
apprenticeship and discipleship.

"It demands very close connections with constituents," and paying
attention to the kinds of training that graduates need for their specific
churches and organizations, says Graham. "We need people who are
formed in certain ways, and that doesn't necessarily happen in courses,
over semesters, with credit hours and grades." The association's standards
draw from lessons about what works at Sioux Falls Seminary and other
early adopters in the field to help encourage quality experimentation
with competency-based education across its member schools, which are
mostly quite small, with a median enrollment of 150 students. "There are
a lot of places and a lot of schools that can benefit from some of the principles and approaches," Graham says, "maybe adapting parts of programs
or adapting some of those methodologies and incorporating them across
the curriculum in some ways."

That sort of sharing of best practices across a discipline or a sector,
with guidance and support from an accreditor and other regulators, is a
big part of how colleges can get assessment right in competency-based
education (or in conventional programs, for that matter). Illinois is a good
example of how this approach can work. The state agency that oversees
higher education, the Illinois Board of Higher Education, has been working with a "coalition of the willing" of more than seventy-five community colleges and four-year institutions, including private colleges, that
are interested in creating competency-based forms of early-childhood
education programs, says Stephanie Bernoteit, the board's executive dep-
uty director.

The agency saw wide variability across institutions. Early-childhood
teaching credentials were being interpreted and assessed differently at
each of the seventy-five institutions across the state that offered them. As
part of an effort to achieve greater agreement and clarity about career
pathways in early-childhood education, the state developed a set of credentials that are designed to be stackable, from high school training up to
graduate degrees. The work led to more interest in defining competencies

and developing assessments. "Fundamentally, what we really want to understand is what people know and can do once they've completed a course at your institution or at my institution," Bernoteit says. "How can we be more clear together about what we expect in the way of those learning outcomes and how we know someone has achieved that?"

The group of institutions decided to work together to start using the same competencies and to consistently describe what the performance of these competencies looks like. The resulting grassroots effort of academics, working with state agencies, managed to translate the system of early-childhood credentials into competencies. The coalition also worked on fundamental questions about assessment—including whether they could co-create valid and reliable assessments, which would be costly to design individually. The group then created a common set of rubrics and a repository of assessments that the state's colleges can use on a voluntary basis. They tapped public and philanthropic dollars to pay for the repository's creation. Faculty members applied for year-long fellowships to help develop the assessments. And the work continues through conferences and workshops, where the faculty developers speak to their peers about what they designed and showcase what the repository makes possible. The assessments in the repository "are not intended to fully subsume every sort of classroom assessment that you as a faculty member might design," Bernoteit says. "But these are intended to support and be a resource, hopefully creating some continuity for you and your transfer partners, among others, about how we're thinking about student learning."

This collaborative approach will lead to more consistent outcomes for students in the state's early-childhood programs. And the coalition will be able to compare competency development across institutions. The result is improvement in the quality of instruction, assessment, and ultimately, early childhood services in Illinois.

Critics of competency-based education may want to relegate it to more vocational skills-based learning. But it is hard to imagine two fields more grounded in complex human interaction than theology and early education. Attempts to improve assessments raise fears among faculty members and students not just because it's hard to get assessments right, but because the process cuts to the core of tough questions about teaching and learning: how do students know when they have grasped the material? Such attempts also lay new responsibility on professors and instructors, as well as colleges themselves, by not just allowing students to slide by with the sort of lackluster performance that might yield a C- grade and a correspondingly limited understanding of the course material and required learning. That's why professional licensure requirements exist—to truly see whether the nursing student can treat a patient or the pilot-in-training can land a plane. If we take history and literature as seriously as these "skills-based" disciplines, and we absolutely should, then we need to take their assessments just as seriously. And while faculty members often want to create their own assessments, which are tied to what they teach, that doesn't mean they are always teaching what's needed for a particular course or competency.

Students in high-quality competency-based programs tend to be engaged rather than intimidated by assessments that require them to master content. Higher education should expect more from students; the soft bigotry of low expectations doesn't feel good on the receiving end. By requiring mastery and proving it with authentic assessment, colleges can help students stay engaged, rather than letting them just get by, and, for far too many, eventually drop out with debt and no credential. Moreover, authentic assessments, unlike publisher-provided testing banks or standardized tests, allow for geographic and culturally informed experiences and frames of reference that can help address issues of relevance and equity. When students can see themselves in the learning, immediately apply their newly mastered skills, and take pride in being genuinely good at something they did not know or were not able to do before, they enjoy the positive impact of personal growth and capacity. It is hard to quantify, but our competency-based degree students often describe secondary effects like quitting smoking, working out, and having more confidence at work. Cramming for an exam and promptly forgetting what was held in short-term memory does not yield the same benefits.

The assessments and required mastery in College for America didn't intimidate Sarema, a mother who earned both associate and bachelor's degrees while working. The degrees helped Sarema advance in her job with the Boston Public Schools. She compared the process to turning in a rough draft of an assignment, which was the standard procedure during her experience in K–12 schools.

> *You felt really good when you got to hear what your professors felt like you could fix. I liked that we were able to never fail. This might be a rough draft, but you get to try again until you pass. That was empowering because often in college we think we'll have a hit or miss. I learned more in those projects and competencies than I did sitting in a lecture hall. And that was simply because the knowledge was given to me, it was up to me to absorb it, and then write about what I took from it.*

Sarema's sentiment was echoed by a peer who participated in a panel in front of the SNHU Board of Trustees. This student described her long-standing math phobia and dread as she started in on the math competencies within a program. She submitted her projects and received "not yet" scores on the rubric, sending her back to dig into the material. Of all the competencies she had to master, this one required the most submissions—though multiple submissions carry no penalty—and she recalled with glee the day she received a "mastery" level:

> *I couldn't just memorize things and take an exam, like my roommates [enrolled in traditional courses] who just forgot everything a day later. I had to really learn. And while I'm not saying I love math now, I know how to do the math I studied and I'm not afraid of it anymore.*

Instead of simply giving this student a passing but poor grade, essentially giving up on her, we encouraged her to keep at it, resubmit, get feedback, and actually learn. By taking time out of the equation and embracing the reality that some things are harder than others, competency-based education requires more student persistence and grit. This approach eliminates the ability to slide by with a poor grade and no real learning, which helps inculcate the sort of integrity that traditional learning models struggle to cultivate through their inadequate assessment practices. The kind of assessment called for in competency-based education is hard, requiring technical skill and that students take the time to really master skills. But it allows us to reframe assessment as a constructive part of the learning activity itself. The "not yet" takes us from "I'm not good at math" to "I'm not *yet* good at math," reflecting what we have learned about growth mindsets and positive psychology.[9] The growth mindset of competency-based education embraces intellectual challenges and views failure as an opportunity to stretch and improve one's abilities. And aside from the secondary psychological benefits mentioned before, research has shown that the sort of positive psychology that is embedded in performance-based assessment also improves student success by increasing engagement and encouraging students to reach their potential strengths.

Most importantly, this type of assessment brings us back to actual student learning, the most essential element of the whole enterprise. Because sound assessment practices can provide us reassurance about what students actually know and can do, we are invited to think more broadly about and innovate around how we design learning to achieve our desired ends, as we will see in the next chapter.

CHAPTER FOUR

DESIGNING
QUALITY PROGRAMS

SHIFTING FROM TIME TO ACTUAL LEARNING as a basis for education forces us to think really, really hard about the claims we make for what students know and can do at the end of their educational experience. We then need to design performance-based assessments that reliably measure their demonstrated mastery of those claims, as we have seen in the previous two chapters. Creating a program thus begins with the *end*, the learning outcomes—desired knowledge and skills—then works backward through program design, questions of what needs to be covered, best content and resources, methods of delivery, and so on. Traditionally, program design has placed greater focus on the curation of content—what content is required for the topics that must be covered. A massive industry dominated by the big textbook publishers exists to supply content. Delivery and experience of the program mostly happen in classrooms, led by faculty. Advances in learning science and instruction in recent years have led to less "sage on the stage" lecturing, with more dynamic and engaging pedagogy becoming common. But walk through the halls of most academic buildings and you'll still see students sitting in rows and a teacher standing at the front of the room in a manner that would not be unfamiliar to a student at the University of Bologna in 1088.

The most exciting thing about a shift to outcomes, backed by rigorous and reliable assessments, is the way it invites new and innovative ways to learn. It prescribes no inputs, no pedagogy, no approach, no methodology. While a focus on measurable outcomes demands clarity about what is being measured, from which no program should ever shy, it doesn't pass judgment on *how* or *where* learning happens, nor on who supports students in that process. In a system that's less parochial about the where and how of learning, we would be better able and more willing to validate learning that students possess when they come to us, whether that learning happened in the military, at work, while still in high school, or in running a family-owned business. We could be more creative in the ways we allow students to demonstrate their learning. For example, we might recognize the genuine knowledge and skills required for a student government treasurer to manage $2 million in funds or for a student athlete to captain the varsity soccer team. We could identify the competencies required, measure student mastery of them, and then count them toward degree completion.

The implications are profound (and perhaps frightening to some in our existing system of education). They include

- a recognition that learning can happen anywhere, and often outside of classrooms and campuses
- an invitation to develop culturally informed curricula that recognize a wider range of what counts as learning, and in which often-marginalized learners can see themselves
- opportunities to dramatically drive down the cost of delivery and, as a result, the cost of a degree
- the breakdown of boundaries between K–12, higher education, and the workforce

- exciting new partnerships and opportunities for different types of providers of learning, as colleges and universities surrender their monopoly on what counts as postsecondary education

None of this means a university cannot continue with the most traditional roles and models of delivery possible. However, making claims for student learning crystal clear and then standing behind those claims through performance-based assessments will test the efficacy of that approach in a way that eludes us now.

When we originally introduced competency-based education to SNHU, the most common misconception I encountered among faculty was a concern that this new focus on measurable outcomes would require them to change their teaching methods or surrender their courses. Some still fear it means their jobs actually go away. None of those things have to be true, though to be fair to faculty members, some of the best-known competency-based programs do take nontraditional approaches to learning, and thus reimagine the role of faculty, as we shall see in the case studies that follow. It is helpful to remember that faculty at teaching institutions do a lot more than meet students in the classroom. This is true in competency-based education as well. Faculty engage in program and course design, curate content, create content, design (or choose) and administer assessments, and advise students. They often have administrative duties, participate in committee work, and, in research universities and even in most teaching-intensive universities, face expectations around scholarship and research.

In the 1960s, the groundbreaking Open University in the UK began to unbundle the instructional roles of faculty, asking them to focus on teaching and their work as subject-matter experts, while putting program design in the hands of teams that included instructional designers, assessment experts, and others, including subject-matter-expert faculty members. (In higher education, faculty subject-matter experts have an advanced degree and deep knowledge in a specific field. They often play an important role in instructional design.) We use the same model in our large online division. The approach has become common in scaled pro-grams where uniform quality across many instances of a single course ("sections" in the parlance of higher education) is far better ensured by a dedicated design team than by individual faculty members. The process we use to develop competency-based programs is illustrated in figure 4.1.

This rigorous procedure brings the right expert in for the right phase of the work. Note, too, that the process starts with the research and iden-tification of competencies, beginning the work with the outcomes sought. Western Governors University, the nation's largest competency-based degree provider (which offers no traditional programs and has no campus), also uses an unbundled approach in its programs, as do many other providers.

Faculty wariness of competency-based education is common since many of the most prominent programs do not preserve traditional fac-ulty roles. These are roles that most faculty members really love, as I did when I was a professor. While the best-known competency-based degree programs substantially alter those traditional roles, a competency-based delivery method of higher education does not actually privilege any learning model. As a result, faculty members have an opportunity to develop models that preserve the functions they most love—or, better yet, that they feel are most valuable to students. If it's direct interaction with students, build the program with that component. If it's in subject-matter expertise, put more emphasis on that aspect of faculty engagement. The test of the model will not be how learning is developed, but in its efficacy. Competency-based education is agnostic on the question of *how* learn-ing happens.

In the spring of 2020, with the pandemic driving unemployment rates not seen since the Great Depression, I asked our faculty to create more affordable options for students. I wanted them to envision programs that would take our tuition from $32,000 to $10,000 annually, be mapped onto competencies, engage students, and have outcomes as good as or better than our traditional programs. At the time of this writing, the first six of those programs have received initial approval, and the faculty are in design mode. All the programs preserve traditional roles for faculty, even if they make less use of traditional classrooms. The academic oversight

FIGURE 4.1

Developing a Competency-Based Program Process Chart

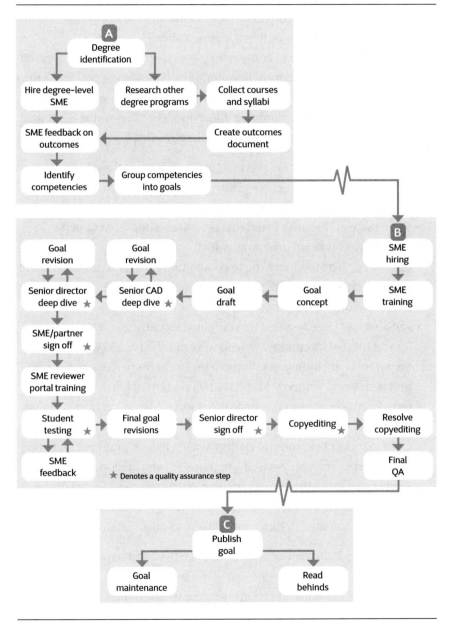

of the programs, a cornerstone of shared governance models, has been preserved and academic freedom has not been constrained. The process hasn't been easy. Many faculty members dislike the change and we are not yet done, but our experience thus far is promising.

Indeed, the new wave of competency-based programs—with approximately 430 institutions actively developing or considering creating a program—is just beginning. Like all disruptive innovations, we are creating, learning, iterating, and improving these models of learning. That said, many new programs are producing excellent results:

- The National Council on Teacher Quality has rated the education college at Western Governors University as the nation's "best value" education school based on its quality and affordability.[1]
- More than ten thousand students have graduated from Capella University's FlexPath programs, which are competency-based and self-paced.[2] The median time to completion for graduates of FlexPath master's degree programs was 42 percent faster than for their peers in credit-hour-based programs.
- Anthem, the large health-care company, recently found big payoffs for the 1,100 of its employees who were enrolled at SNHU's College for America, including that participants were more likely to be promoted at work. A survey found that 93 percent of participants preferred CFA to traditional college programs while 88 percent said that the program gave a boost to their view of Anthem as an employer.
- Ohio's Sinclair Community College used a federal grant to create flexibly paced competency-based programs in information technology.[3] Students in those programs are substantially more likely to complete those courses than their peers, are earning credentials at three times the speed, and are ten times more likely to do an internship.

We recently launched an effort to design the third iteration of College for America, which incorporates what we learned from earlier versions of the program. As Clay Christensen's research reminds us, the quality improvement curve for disruptive innovations is steeper and faster than it is for the incumbent models it disrupts (see figure 4.2).

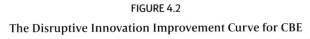

FIGURE 4.2

The Disruptive Innovation Improvement Curve for CBE

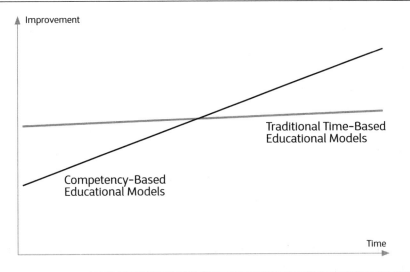

If the time-based systems of federal financial aid can better accommodate non-time-based programs (see chapter 5 for a proposed model) and accreditors can make more space for innovation, program development and improvement could be further accelerated. In the meantime, here is a sample of exciting programs that are already up and running, and that illustrate the power of educational approaches untethered to time and focused on assessment of student learning.

WESTERN GOVERNORS UNIVERSITY

The nation's largest competency-based university began in the mid-1990s with the search for answers to a growing problem: how can we ensure that working adults have greater access to a college education that fits their schedule?

Western Governors University (WGU) was an attempt by a group of governors of nineteen western states to answer that question. The university's founding mission was to overcome barriers of time and space that were (and are) preventing millions of residents of their states from pursuing a college degree. Bringing together the newly viable internet with the idea of competency-based education, which remained relatively unknown at the time, the governors knew a different form of higher education could become a reality. Roy Romer, who was then the Democratic governor of Colorado, helped lead the bipartisan team of governors who started WGU. He later said:

> *Universities measure the wrong thing. They measure time. They measure prestige. I wanted to base a degree on performance—and that was a real revolution.*

After receiving initial funding from government, foundations, and private industry, the fully online and nonprofit university was up and running in 1999. Its first programs were in information technology and education. The early years weren't easy, as is typically the case for any disruptive innovation. Because of its national scope, Western Governors had to get approval from four regional accreditors, a major, time-consuming lift. Meanwhile, the university was running low on its startup money. Much of the problem was the administrative bureaucracy of a time-based higher education system that didn't work for the students WGU wanted to reach. Mike Leavitt, the former Republican governor of Utah who helped spearhead the university's creation, later said:

> *We had to reinvent an alternative process, not to replace traditional higher education, but to supplement, to serve populations that were not properly served by the existing system. We believe that this new, more innovative approach to higher education needed to include both new technology and a fundamental shift in what we measure. Overcoming thousands of years of tradition is no small task, and higher education has essentially thought the same way about the learning process for a long time.*

Sound familiar? Those challenges still exist, of course. But WGU showed they can be overcome, and how. After years of quiet, steady growth, the university enrolled 130,000 students in 2020. Fully 70 percent of its students come from underserved backgrounds. And 40 percent are first-generation college students. Among its many positive outcomes, the university's alumni give it very high marks, particularly on perceptions of value and results in the job market. WGU graduates are, on average, about 20 percentage points more likely to be employed full time than are graduates of other colleges, according to a nationally representative survey of college alumni conducted by Gallup.[4] They are also more likely to work in jobs that relate to their undergraduate majors; to like their jobs; and to be thriving in their social, financial, and physical well-being. Alumni of Western Governors are also more than twice as likely to strongly agree that their education was worth the cost (72 percent) compared to graduates of other private, nonprofit institutions (31 percent). The average annual tuition for a student pursuing a bachelor's degree at WGU is $6,670, roughly half the national average tuition of $12,775. And annual tuition for a master's degree from the university is $7,405, a fraction of the national average of $36,832. As a result, 42 percent of undergraduates at the university complete their degrees without taking on student loans, with average debt loads of about $15,000, which is roughly half the national average. Tuition also is offered at a flat rate, meaning that students are able to complete as many competencies as they can for the same price during a six-month term.

The university's four colleges cover business, health professions, teacher training, and IT, in that order of popularity with students. All of its programs feature deep relationships with employers, which helps to make the credentials it issues more workforce relevant. And WGU prioritizes having a personal touch with students. Genevieve Kirch was the university's first graduate, completing a master's degree in learning and technology one year after WGU opened its virtual doors. Shortly thereafter she wrote to the university's then president:

Many times the concern and care expressed by the WGU personnel made a tremendous difference in my life. At times when the going was

rough, I knew there were others out there pulling for me. This is a credit
to the WGU format. In a school environment it is fairly easy to fade
into the woodwork. With WGU you are the focal point, and it is hard
to not notice the supreme care.[5]

Despite the enthusiasm of alumni, WGU has had to overcome plenty of resistance from higher education's incumbent system. Bill Simmons, a former government relations representative for the university, once cited the "real negative reaction that this was going to threaten everything that higher education stood for." To be fair, critics were right to worry. The university does indeed challenge many of the academy's flawed assumptions. For starters, students don't fail there. "It's not even a word at WGU," says Marni Baker Stein, the university's provost and chief academic officer. "It's not transcripted until you pass it." This approach is at the core of WGU, which is built around the student's personalized pathway toward mastery. And while the university is not completely untethered from the credit hour, it prioritizes flexibility for students in their pursuit of competencies and avoids a structural focus on courses, credits, or even degrees. That central principle extends to the university's innovative approach to instruction and assessment. "We organize around individual student journeys," says Baker Stein.

To make this approach work, the university divides the traditional faculty role into three different roles, in part because WGU says no single faculty member could properly execute all the required tasks. Its roughly 4,500 faculty members include program mentors, course instructors, and evaluators. Each new student is assigned a program mentor when first enrolled. Mentors are experts in the field who work with the student up front to create a term plan that is personalized to fit the student's life and goals. They work with students until graduation, giving guidance and program instruction throughout, as well as information on university programs, policies, and procedures. Mentors also assess students' strengths and development needs to help them create a study plan.

Course instructors at WGU are subject-matter experts with advanced degrees in the courses they instruct. This group helps students create their personalized course plans, focusing on making sure they get the right amount of faculty support. They provide instruction both proactively and reactively, offering online one-to-one discussions and group forums to students.

The final group of faculty members is the subject-matter experts who evaluate assessments to determine if students have demonstrated competency. These evaluators hold doctoral degrees or other postgraduate certifications in the areas they evaluate. A key part of their work is to provide quick, personalized feedback on submissions from students—usually within twenty-four hours and always within seventy-two hours. Evaluators remain anonymous when giving feedback. Because they do not otherwise interact with students or develop curricula or assessments, the university stresses that these faculty members can focus on student performance while being free of bias or other barriers to a fair and timely evaluation. This arrangement helps WGU avoid the conflict of interest we see in faculty grading in conventional higher education.

Good assessments are crucial in competency-based education, and Western Governors is no exception. Beyond the three types of faculty members who work with students on instruction, support, and evaluation, the university employs faculty who specialize in the development of assessments and curricula. "We are first and foremost an identifier and a designer of assessments," says Baker Stein.

For any field of study offered by the university, WGU works closely with employers to determine the most in-demand skills in those disciplines. Its faculty teams fit those skills into competencies, which are stacked up into "playlists" of competencies. The playlists are then progressively combined to become degree programs—all with job skills at the center. This sort of reverse engineering makes degree programs valuable in the job market but remains all too rare in higher education.

Students take a readiness assessment at the beginning of the term for each course. (Terms are six months long, and students can begin a degree program on the first day of any month.) After completing the readiness assessment, students work with their mentors to determine an estimated time to mastery for required competencies. The resulting plan is flexible, and the student's schedule can be tweaked depending on the speed of their progress, or when unexpected time, money, or other problems force them to hit pause on their studies. Students are deemed competent by evaluators through the assessment of their submitted work, usually in the form of papers or projects. All told, the university conducts 127,000 assessment evaluations per month, 50,000 of which are administered and proctored via webcam.[6]

WGU's scale allows it to do many things other institutions can't do in competency-based education. For example, a 2015 analysis found that WGU's relatively low tuition rates tend to work best for programs with at least six thousand students enrolled, meaning that smaller programs might need to have higher tuition rates to break even.[7] Yet the university's status as an industry leader has led to imitation by many institutions, including ones with fundamentally different business models. And while higher education's traditionalists may have been the most resistant to WGU in its early days, the ones who probably should have been worried were the leaders of big for-profit college chains. The *Washington Monthly* was prescient, with a 2011 article titled "The College For-Profits Should Fear," which said, "By offering adults an education that is faster, cheaper, and better than the likes of Kaplan, Phoenix, or Capella, the nonprofit Western Governors University just might eat their lunch."[8] A decade later, as the for-profit sector continues to lose students and revenue, WGU keeps on growing and producing thousands of satisfied graduates.

SINCLAIR COMMUNITY COLLEGE/ SALT LAKE COMMUNITY COLLEGE

The typical community college student is twenty-eight years old, holds down a job, and attends college part time.[9] Fully half are people of color, and Latinos comprise more than a quarter of the sector's total enrollment. Among the millions of lower-income community college students who receive federal Pell Grants, about half work more than twenty hours per week.[10] As a result of work and family responsibilities, time is a scarce resource for community college students, who account for 45 percent of American undergraduates. Most will leave college—often several times— without completing a degree, and just 40 percent earn a degree or certificate within six years after enrolling.

These challenges have worsened during the pandemic. And the overbooked lives of community college students have contributed to the sector's severe enrollment decline during the last year. Experts say time is the biggest reason why competency-based education's flexible approach, particularly when coupled with prior learning assessment, holds great promise for community college students. "The model theoretically has potential and can come to fruition at scale," says Debra Bragg, a consultant and fellow at New America who has evaluated competency-based programs at community colleges.

That potential has largely been unrealized thus far, however, mostly due to the lack of resources at perpetually cash-strapped community colleges. Yet a $2.5 billion federal grant program from the Labor Department during the Obama administration gave a glimpse of what might be possible in the two-year-degree sector.[11] The grants were designed to help community colleges prepare students for jobs in fast-growing industries. They funded programs that were geared to adult students who needed college programs to be on accelerated timelines because of pressure they were feeling to quickly enter or rejoin the workforce to support their families. Sinclair Community College, which is located in Dayton, Ohio, led a consortium of community colleges that used the federal grant money to work with Western Governors to develop competency-based programs at their institutions. More than a million Ohioans hold some college credits and no degree. And the "business as usual" approach of trying to serve those learners just wasn't cutting it, according to Christina Amato, Sinclair's dean of eLearning. The $12 million federal grant to the consortium kickstarted Sinclair's experimentation with competency-based education back in 2012, beginning with IT instruction aimed at veterans of the US military and other adult students. Since then, Sinclair has created seventy-seven competency-based courses and thirteen full programs. Roughly four thousand students have been educated in those programs, and Sinclair has advised scores of other colleges in how to create high-quality competency-based learning pathways.

The pandemic has given a boost to Sinclair's ambitions, says Amato. "COVID has presented some unique opportunities to evaluate where we need to go with competency-based education," she says. "Where there may have been mindset obstacles a year ago, our faculty are much more open to the digital teaching and learning space than they were before. So, it's time to think ahead to be bigger and bolder with competency-based education."

Experiments the two-year college is working on include

- integrating strategies for competency-based education and prior-learning assessment to create a seamless "credit for what you know" initiative for learners with life experience
- using competency-based education as the launch platform for a digital project to ditch static transcripts and instead use dynamic learning records (with more student ownership and autonomy) that outline competencies rather than full courses
- stacking developmental (or remedial) education courses with the next sequenced college-level course in the same term, which would allow students to finish both courses at their own pace within a term
- offering blended in-person and online competency-based courses (which has previously been challenging in the community college environment)
- using machine learning in competency-based courses to assess a student's level of knowledge more accurately, so as to better place them within a course

Amato is blunt when asked what will help Sinclair achieve its ambitious goals:

Money. That's the honest answer. We have all of the talent and expertise necessary on the academic and eLearning side. But faculty and eLearning are already so overloaded, it's hard to imagine we could pile on one more thing. Being able to fully release faculty and staff to build these things would be critically necessary for any traction.

Salt Lake Community College (SLCC) also received one of the Obama administration grants and used it to create noncredit competency-based certificates in its career and technical education programs. With a total enrollment of roughly 40,000 students, the college is the largest and most diverse institution in Utah. SLCC had previously tried competency-based education, but the federal grant allowed the college to develop more modern and innovative versions, moving away from seat-time, clock hours, and face-to-face instruction. The new programs were designed for students to master industry-focused competencies and to use their credentials to get living-wage jobs. The college exceeded its enrollment goals for the project, with 1,114 students eventually enrolling in the competency-based programs.

Students on average completed much more quickly than is typical in the corresponding traditional credential tracks, says Eric Heiser, a former dean at the college who helped lead the project and is now the provost at Central Ohio Technical College. When surveyed, students said the flexibility of the competency-based programs was the biggest benefit. That meant being able to move faster through competencies where students brought relevant knowledge and experience to the table. But Heiser says it was even more important to students that the program allowed them to slow down when they needed to—because they were struggling with a competency or had to dial back their studies when life events got in the way:

> These are students who are hanging on the edge. They are one flat tire away from dropping out of college. If they're in a traditional, fifteen-week, cohort-based course, and they miss a week because their kid was sick, they're done. They're out and they're not coming back. And we've already seen that, and the data is proving that in COVID-specific terms.

The college faced a mountain of red tape in getting the programs approved for federal financial aid, Heiser says. For example, SLCC had to create a time-clock system to let students punch in and out, so they could prove they were present for the required number of clock hours. In addition, Bragg says some faculty members were skeptical about the program.

But with strong support from the college's leadership and the guidance of Heiser and his team, the competency-based programs achieved what Bragg calls a "miraculous transformation" and were up and running relatively quickly.

For more two-year colleges to follow Sinclair and SLCC's lead, Bragg says they should consider housing the programs outside of the conventional institution. "Colleges often try to wedge it into existing higher-ed systems," she says. Heiser says student success coaches and advisors are crucial to making competency-based education work at community colleges. That takes money, of course. And finding outside funding is a priority in the sector, whether from the feds, private foundations, or states. Heiser says specially budgeted funds from Utah's state government were crucial to the project's success. "We were able to build our own staff with that extra money," he says. "Had we not had that money it wouldn't have been possible."

LIPSCOMB UNIVERSITY

No single institution or program has a monopoly on how competency-based education should look. The approach is agnostic on questions of delivery methods, as long as institutions can stand behind their claims about student learning. This opens the door to experimentation and iteration.

Lipscomb University's competency-based programs have changed substantially since 2013, when they first gained approval from an accreditor. The small, private, religiously affiliated university in Nashville initially designed its competency-based programs for working adults who brought previously earned college credits and plenty of on-the-job experience when they enrolled. The competency-based programs were offered in-person only, and featured a groundbreaking assessment center, where students went through an intensive in-person evaluation for their prior learning and skills. These days almost all of the university's competency-based programs are fully online, with asynchronous courses that students can take at their own pace. And the students have changed as well, with more traditional-aged students enrolled, as well as a growing number of students who want full degree programs rather than ones aimed mostly at degree completion.

The assessment center is still a key part of the competency-based programs offered by the College of Professional Studies at Lipscomb. But students are not required to go through that prior-learning assessment, and the university is working to create a fully virtual version of it. Lipscomb also now offers an eight-hour simulation that uses a behavioral assessment model to measure fifteen distinct competencies, all tied to specific core workplace competencies, which are linked to up to thirty university credits undergraduates can earn and six credits for graduate students.[12] Lipscomb has found that students who participate in the simulation are 27 percent more likely to persist in their programs and 2.5 times more likely to graduate, with 92 percent of those who participate graduating in a year or less. The university remains focused on assessing students' previously earned knowledge, skills, and abilities; they've just found more ways to do it. "Honoring, in all of what we do, what students bring to the experience, is part of a key goal that we have," says Susan Galbreath, Lipscomb's senior vice president for strategy.

The program's strength is combining the flexibility of asynchronous courses with regular access to a real professor, through video announcements or in virtual calls and chats. Students tend to react well to this blend, whether they're a nineteen-year-old, first-time student or a bank president who enrolled to complete her unfinished degree and who moved more quickly through the program than most students. The range of options and the asynchronous courses have also helped Lipscomb adapt to the pandemic. For example, the university offers competency-based versions of corresponding programs from its conventional campus. And hundreds of traditional-aged students have enrolled in those online courses to avoid campus and to take advantage of having more time for their coursework during COVID-19 lockdowns. Many students have been able to "binge watch" their way through online course material from the competency-based programs. Galbreath says 525 of the university's 2,900 traditional undergraduates were taking at least one of its asynchronous online courses during the spring term of 2021. These students found their way to the competency-based programs on their own, without having been recruited, after Lipscomb made the option available the previous term. Galbreath says:

> They will be able to finish that class as quickly as they can. And they will still have gained the academic credential and the knowledge that's necessary for them to progress to the next level. And that lightens my heart. At the same time, it's burdened by knowing that there are 2,900 sitting over here in a time-pressed situation that they can't change. So, we're glad to be partnering right now with the mothership in a way that would not have happened if COVID had not happened. It just has busted at the seams and there is no putting this genie in the bottle.

Officials at Lipscomb say they have yet to encounter a major that doesn't work well in a competency-based, online format, with the exception of pharmacy and other disciplines where programmatic accreditors impose specific industry requirements (because they can't trust conventional grading). So far, the university has created parallel competency-based versions of psychology, public administration, English, math, chemistry, lab sciences, and more. And Lipscomb now offers a full competency-based general education curriculum that mirrors the traditional one. A popular virtual course among the university's undergraduates, for example, is a competency-based version of physical education, where students must put together their own five-week wellness plan.

The university has faced some resistance to the virtual tracks from faculty members, often because of their broader skepticism of online education rather than competency-based learning in particular, a position that's harder to justify amid the national pivot to online education. Emily Smith, associate dean of academics for Lipscomb's online programs, says:

> We've been strategic in getting a lot of the traditional faculty members to teach in our program, which is the best way to convert them and have some of them become almost evangelical about the modality.

Lipscomb has also tapped faculty members from the traditional side of the university to serve as liaisons with their corresponding competency-based program. Their job is to help ensure that the competency-based courses and programs mirror the learning on the conventional side, and to bring their voice and experience back to their peers. That cross pollination has helped with faculty buy-in.

Students at Lipscomb can now move back and forth between the competency-based and the traditional sides, taking courses from either. Both operations use the same student information system, a recent improvement, and all students will soon use the same learning management system. Even with these attempts to make the competency-based programs seamless for traditional students at the university, some have remained skeptical, Galbreath says. And while internal bureaucracies previously hindered the university from doing more recruiting of students beyond campus, the bigger challenge is that the modality just looks so different. "CBE is hard to explain," Galbreath says. "We have to work really hard to not look like we're cutting corners, to not look like we are a cheaper, less quality alternative."

The programs remain small, with about 230 students enrolled fully in competency-based tracks. But growth has been picking up, with 7–10 percent increases in recent terms. And Lipscomb has recently created free, noncredit versions of competency-based and virtual courses, which have drummed up interest in the programs. For example, during the pandemic the university allowed displaced hospitality workers to audit a free version of a course in applied organizing and planning, part of its hospitality and entertainment management degree program. More than 200 students enrolled. To help students better understand competency-based education and its benefits as they mull whether to take the leap, Lipscomb has created videos where a narrator succinctly describes how the programs work, stressing that the courses are tailored to students, with the end goal of competencies coming first:

> *Your professor and other experts in the content made some decisions about the most important competencies in the content of the course.*

They thought about what they would want you to be able to do when you finish, not just what you can hold in your mind for a few hours. They articulated these big ideas and defined competencies around them. Then, they determined what assessment would show that you have attained the competencies—a paper, a project, a speech, a test, etc.—and they created a rubric that shows what competent work looks like. Then they created learning opportunities for you to complete at your own pace that will help you get to that competent performance.

Imagine this like a piano recital. You know the pieces you will have to play at the end, and when the deadline is. You know how well you have to play them and to get there, you will have to practice different parts of the piece and get feedback from your instructor. It does not matter if you do poorly the first time, or the second, or the twenty-second time you try it. Your bad grades will not follow you through the course. They are just feedback that tells you what you need to work on. All that matters is that you eventually will get to the recital and be able to play the music well. However, in our recital, you get the chance of doing it over if you mess up the first time. So, the final is not that stressful.

NORTHERN ARIZONA UNIVERSITY

Innovation can be a heavier lift at public universities than at private institutions. As state institutions, public universities typically feature a different level of bureaucracy, which tends to slow down attempts to rethink how to deliver higher education. Yet public institutions also have a mandate to serve the citizens of their state, including working adults who are unable to attend a residential campus on a fixed schedule.

Northern Arizona University (NAU) is one of several public institutions that have been pioneers in competency-based education. The university, which enrolls more than thirty thousand students, first introduced competency-based undergraduate degrees in 2013. Other notable public universities in the space include the University of Maine, Presque Isle, which offers several online, competency-based degrees at a flat tuition rate over eight-week sessions, and the University of Wisconsin System's Flexible Option, which features several direct assessment (meaning untethered from time) degree programs through three campuses.

NAU's personalized learning division now includes five undergraduate and two graduate programs that are competency-based, including degrees in liberal arts, computer information technology, nursing, management, and small business administration. The computer information and nursing credentials also feature a competency-based pipeline from bachelor's to master's degrees. Tuition for the degree programs and their six-month terms is subscription based and covers all the competencies students can complete in the term. The rate of $3,000 for six months ($3,750 in nursing), which includes textbooks and all other university fees, is substantially more affordable than tuition for NAU's conventional programs, which are priced at roughly $6,000 per term for in-state students.

Corrine Gordon, an associate professor of English at Northern Arizona and the academic program chair for NAU Online, says the university decided to take the plunge with competency-based education to bring learning possibilities to more working students who hold some college credits but no credential:

> There are so many learners who have quite a bit of college experience—maybe a history class at this community college, an English class at that college. We wanted to give them a place where they could take those disparate credits and course completions, bring them together, and accelerate their time to degree completion by honoring as much of their transfer credit as we could. We have multiple options for the learner. What's going to be the best fit? It's not a better or worse option, it's another option.

The university has made adjustments to the programs over the last eight years, drawing from lessons about what works well and what can be improved. Competency-based education done right requires fundamental changes to traditional university practices, including deeply ingrained administrative structures and faculty roles. And while a culture of continuous academic improvement is a mantra in higher education, and even a requirement by accreditors, it is far from the norm.

NAU's competency-based programs were created through backward design, starting with defining competencies and then embedding them in a framework that sits inside the course structure. Like many other competency-based programs, NAU features a digital dashboard that is synched up with its student information and learning management systems, to give students a visual representation of how far along they are in mastering competencies on their way to completion. This sort of positive feedback can be a powerful motivator. It's the same kind of thinking that a growing number of conventional college programs are using to boost student success by focusing on the academic momentum of students in their first couple years of enrollment.[13] This focus can include helping to ensure that students take enough credits in their first year, making sure they complete gateway courses in math and English early on, and even awarding associate degrees when they are halfway to a bachelor's. The dashboard at NAU links competencies to courses, which Gordon says helps students reap the benefits of competency-based education while seeing that their mastery of competencies is leading to college credit. "The students really love the flexibility," says Gordon. "They like that they get to set the pacing."

Students who are enrolled in the university's competency-based nursing programs can move between three available formats—online, face-to-face, and competency versions. "If you find that you're in the wrong format, we can transition you to a different one," says Gordon. But such a move is more complicated in other competency-based programs at the university, largely because of time-based logistical hurdles in NAU's administrative and technology systems. In the early days, Gordon says the competency-based programs faced scaling challenges because much of the necessary administrative work couldn't be automated—including financial aid, enrollment management, and more. "When we broke all the rules, we had a lot of manual pieces that went with that," she says.

After the first year, the university got approval for students to receive federal financial aid in competency-based programs. But some students overenrolled in competencies early in the programs, threatening to hit federal limits for their financial aid eligibility and jeopardizing their longer-term access to aid. So the university created benchmarking and "gentle guardrails" for students so they could more easily avoid problems with their aid eligibility.

NAU has ambitious goals about how many learners it can reach with competency-based degrees. The current enrollment across the programs is 650 students, which has been flat for about four years. Years ago, the university advertised for its competency-based degrees in an in-flight airline magazine. "That was when I saw our growth really rocket," Gordon says. "And then, for fiscal reasons, they stopped pursuing that approach." While the programs could benefit from more attempts by the university to get the word out, diverting money from the main campus for marketing is a big lift at a public university with relatively tight budgets. That challenge is even more profound for smaller regional public universities and community colleges.

The Education Department requires instructors in competency-based education programs to have "regular and substantive" interaction with students, including contact initiated by the instructor. This requirement has long been a source of confusion for the field, and the federal government tried to clarify it in 2020.[14] When NAU launched its competency-based programs, the university tapped senior faculty members to work as mentors to students, in part to comply with the regular-and-substantive rules. Those highly credentialed professors spent most of their time advising students, and very little in helping to design and oversee the instructional model. While most faculty members liked the mentor role, Gordon says they weren't as skilled at it as they were with instruction and assessment. So the university decided to tap its advising team for the mentoring, freeing up veteran faculty to focus on their strengths.

NAU also changed its take on the faculty role in competency-based programs. It began with a disaggregated model like the one Western Governors employs. That approach worked well on many fronts, Gordon says. But she says it also had drawbacks for students and the program:

We have moved back over to a space in the middle, toward the tradi-
tional side, where it's really the same faculty who are doing the instruc-
tion and the assessment. We found that it wasn't that useful for us to
divorce those pieces of the role. We found that the two together made
the most sense. As a teacher and having been a curriculum person
myself, when you've worked with a student on the instructional piece
and then are able to assess their understanding, their competency, I
have a stronger sense as an educator than just coming in blind to an
assessment that's black and white. So we moved back to that more tra-
ditional space.

That shift has worked well for the university. And it is another example
of how competency-based education offers plenty of flexibility depending
on the widely diverging needs of students and the institutions that serve
them. As NAU's competency-based offerings have matured, Gordon says
the university has gotten savvier about "demystifying" how the programs
can and should work—for faculty members and administrators as well
as students. The engagement with students is similar to what occurs in
traditional programs, as are the outcomes. "It's just a parallel space that's
not better or worse, just an alternative based on what a student needs
and wants," says Gordon. Competency-based education isn't ideal for all
students or instructors at NAU. But the university gets rave reviews about
the program from the many students who are a good fit for the self-paced,
affordable programs.

Gordon has a background in teaching theater. She draws on that experience when describing to her peers how competency-based education
works, particularly in the liberal arts:

Really it doesn't matter to me if you've seen Hamlet, read Hamlet, or if
you've worked with King Lear, or if you've worked with Hamilton. The
question is not "tell me about Hamlet or Hamilton." The question is
"how do you apply this understanding of literary analysis or produc-
tion evaluations? How do you apply that to whatever text you have in
front of you?" From a competency-based education standpoint, it's all
about the skillset, the ability. By me giving you a play to analyze, what

is it I'm hoping you'll take or read into it or see? From that perspective I feel like liberal arts is one of the easiest fields to do in competency-based education. A college education does not, in and of itself, mean that my transcripts are going to say X, Y, Z. It means that I'm skilled and able to do work at that next level—the professional level or the next level of schooling. It's a demonstration of readiness.

FREEDOM AND ACCOUNTABILITY

In these four examples of competency-based degree programs, and the many others available but not mentioned here, we find variety, creativity, and innovation in delivery, as well as demonstrably strong results. They are characterized by clarity around student outcomes and thoughtful, robust assessment of student success in achieving those outcomes. And these programs reframe the concept of academic struggle, captured well by Lipscomb's invitation for students to keep trying and WGU's rejection of the concept of failure. When we have a system that focuses on these parts of the educational equation, we are free to rethink how we design learning and to reconsider its component parts.

Criticism of competency-based education usually starts with a grudging allowance that these programs may be fine for the teaching of skills, but not for genuine knowledge. Or, as one critic put it, "just learning to perform a series of designated tasks, like a team on *The Amazing Race*."[15] However, as outlined in chapter 2, competency-based programs can powerfully reinvigorate disciplines in the humanities by more clearly identifying the valuable knowledge and skills possessed by graduates in English, philosophy, and history. Because competency-based education does not prescribe, it makes no argument for a particular program design or delivery method, nor for their structures. It does not

- advocate for or against any form of faculty governance
- lead to more or less academic freedom
- validate or prohibit any role involved with the delivery of programs
- speak to how much or little to involve technology

- demand any particular setting or venue for learning
- require a specific structure for delivery bound to time, place, or granularity of the learning (though as we will see in the next chapter, federal financial aid imposes structure)

From a program design perspective, a competency-based approach provides new freedom to explore the design and delivery of learning. Programs can be developed by faculty in the most traditional of shared governance models or designed in a more top-down way with little faculty control. I have seen our competency-based programs delivered in traditional classrooms, but also on a playground in a crime-ridden neighborhood and in refugee camps. Programs can be structured around courses or without them, as we have seen in the cases described here. They can include traditional roles for faculty or embrace alternative mentoring, design, and instructional faculty roles.

This very freedom frightens traditionalists because it allows for the development of educational programs unlike the ones that they experienced and that worked so well for them. If these skeptics work within higher education, it also allows for programs that may or may not embrace their role. Faculty feel especially vulnerable, as they have seen a steep decline in tenure-track positions, increasing use of part-time faculty, and growing criticism of their traditional role in shared governance. While competency-based education does not argue for any of those shifts, the possibility that new models might hasten them or further erode the centrality of faculty to higher education is genuinely threatening. Especially if these models work better than traditionally designed programs, at least for some significant portion of students. In the current system, based on inputs, faculty can at least argue that their role is critical. In an outcomes-based system, there is a chance that high-quality programming can occur without traditional faculty roles. While perhaps hard to accept, innovation and technology are dramatically altering the roles of highly trained professionals in most fields, and higher education will not be an exception.

The cost of all that freedom in program design is accountability, as we have seen in chapters 2 and 3. In competency-based education programs, the claims made for student learning will have to be clear, transparent, and measurable. The assessments that test those claims will have to be performance-based, valid and reliable, and rigorous. While these core tenets of competency-based education allow for genuine assessment of student learning, they also hold institutions and their programs (as well as their people) accountable in ways that are not accomplished in the learning outcomes movement that has been widely adopted in higher education and is sometimes confused with competency-based education. Under the outcomes approach, which is typically required by accreditors, faculty members determine what their students should be learning and how to measure that learning. The movement has helpfully brought more focus on what graduates have ostensibly learned. But outcomes are often bland generalities complemented by inadequate assessment, far short of what competency-based education requires. The Century Foundation's Robert Shireman, a former Education Department official during the Obama administration, offers a stinging critique of the outcomes movement and argues for *more* emphasis on the credit hour and reliance on faculty.[16] While Shireman would backtrack to the flawed credit hour, largely focusing on a traditional residential campus model that only serves a minority of today's students, and reverting to traditional pedagogy as the best means of delivering programs, he at least calls for more evidence of genuine student learning:

> *An accountability approach that starts with the artifacts of student engagement stands the best chance of prompting institutional redesigns that will increase low-income students' likelihood of graduation, with a high-quality degree.*

Collecting a range of student learning artifacts (objects created by students during their instruction) will provide some insight into the kinds of work students are doing, but little meaningful understanding of what they know and can do with their learning.

Competency-based education has the twin virtues of opening up higher education to new program models and their delivery along with genuine measures of student learning. We can be more innovative and more accountable. In a set of interviews SNHU conducted with young learners in Los Angeles, all Generation Z and low-income students of color, the one theme that ran throughout like a refrain was, "I hate school, but I love learning." We can create new ways of learning for digital natives graduating high school, who are tired of our industrial-age models of learning and need the right knowledge and skills to thrive in a world far more complex than the one in which I grew up. For their parents, who could never access our system or who did and then never completed, we can create programs that capture the learning they gained along the way, that fit their overburdened lives both in terms of cost and time, and that help them get the credentials they need to unlock opportunity. When we finally measure quality based on actual mastery of outcomes, we can unleash the creativity and passion of educators trapped in tired institutional and programmatic models. But to do this in our regulated industry, we must also reform the ways we provide financial assistance to low-income students, the subject of the following chapter.

CHAPTER FIVE

RETHINKING FEDERAL
FINANCIAL AID

HOW WILL I PAY FOR IT? This is the most difficult and important question the vast majority of Americans face when mulling whether to attend college. More than 80 percent of first-time, full-time students receive some form of federal financial aid so they can pursue a credential that has become a prerequisite for entering the middle class. As a result, federal spending is the oxygen that keeps higher education alive as an industry. The aid goes to students, funneled through college and university financial aid systems. The institutions take the portion that covers tuition, fees, and other direct costs and then give the students any remaining aid funds as a refund to cover other indirect costs of attendance, like books, gas money, and more.

Because our higher education system is based on a measure of time, the federal financial aid apparatus that was developed to support college students shares those time-based contours. As a result, enormously complex administrative processes for the disbursement of student aid have arisen around the flawed currency of credit hours, a measure of time instead of actual learning.* A badly needed fix to these deeply entrenched structures won't be easy. But our federal financial aid system enables the government to launch demonstration projects and experimental sites to test new and innovative approaches for financial aid. A demonstration project could feature quality controls to protect students and taxpayers while creating a laboratory for colleges and other providers to move beyond the shackles of time—time being a resource poor Americans lack. Lessons learned from the demonstration could be used to prototype and test a financial aid system that aligns with, and thus supports, competency-based education.

Developing this framework for an aid system based on student learning rather than the credit hour would help competency-based education thrive. But that's dramatically understating the ripple effects of such an experiment. The rebooted aid system I describe in this chapter could be a new GI Bill for the American worker, one that would empower colleges and universities to finally realize their mission of expanding opportunity, rather than helping to perpetuate inequity. The benefits would be felt by students, particularly the vulnerable ones we've failed for far too long, as well as faculty members, colleges themselves, and society as a whole. It would be less susceptible to the kinds of abuses that consumer protection advocates fear, while better focusing institutional attention on student success and completion. Because federal financial aid is complex, in this chapter we will go in depth on policy details and get a little wonky. But the details are what enable and constrain reform in a regulated industry like higher education. So strap in.

In 2013, when the US Department of Education approved Southern New Hampshire to offer the nation's debut direct assessment degree

---

*The Administrative Procedure Act (APA) of 1946 governs the process by which federal agencies develop and issue regulations. It includes requirements for publishing notices of proposed and final rule making in the Federal Register, and provides opportunities for the public to comment on notices of proposed rule making.

program, the first degree program to be untethered from the credit hour, we were excited to offer a program designed around genuine and rigorous measures of student learning. At least until we tried to apply financial aid.

The regulatory language of Title IV of the Higher Education Act held out great promise:

> *(1) A direct assessment program is an instructional program that, <u>in lieu of credit hours or clock hours</u> [emphasis mine] as a measure of student learning, utilizes direct assessment of student learning, or recognizes the direct assessment of student learning by others. The assessment must be consistent with the accreditation of the institution or program utilizing the results of the assessment.*

The regulatory language goes on to focus on what students know and can do and gives examples of the evidence that might be used in assessment: artifacts such as papers, portfolios, and performance. However, the department's rules still required non-time-based programs like ours to calculate financial aid based on measures of time.

Effective federal policy making typically requires legislation to be debated in very public ways. But the impact of an enacted policy can be amplified or muted by administrative rules that are later developed to support it. That happens through a process of "negotiated rule making," public hearings in which administrative rule changes are surfaced and discussed. Then the federal agency issues a final set of rules for how the legislation will work. If a presidential administration and the government agency want to amplify the impact of legislation, the administrative rules can do so. However, they can also be crafted to constrain or reduce the impact of new legislation. If legislation creates a body of law, administrative rules breathe life into that body. Or not. With direct assessment, it is not clear if Education Department staff members simply failed to get the necessary administrative rules in place to support direct assessment or if they preferred not to do so.

The *legislative* language of the Higher Education Act, allowing for an alternative to time, invited a fundamental rethinking of learning models such as the one for which we were approved. But the underlying *administrative* language of the federal financial aid system was as bound up as ever in measures of time, not learning. Time is present everywhere in those rules, which define things like the academic year, minimum weeks of instruction, satisfactory academic progress (measured across time), and more. While lawmakers envisioned academic programs in which learning might be directly measured in lieu of credit or clock hours, the machinery of our financial aid system made it impossible to fully realize that vision. For example, the new approval process for direct assessment programs like ours included these requirements for explaining the administration of federal aid:

- how you determined the minimum weeks of instructional time
- how you define the payment period
- how you will document that an academic activity takes place on a weekly basis
- how the student will interact with a faculty member on a regular and substantive basis
- how you define a full-time student[1]

Trying to square a program not based on time with administration of aid that remains firmly tied to time made the management of financial aid even more complicated than it already was for existing programs (and that is saying a lot). Not surprisingly, very few other institutions followed our lead in creating non-time-based or direct assessment programs. If we want a new form of higher education, one that is more equitable, better suited for the time-constrained lives of low-income learners, and designed for a world in which students will dip in and out of a learning ecosystem throughout their lives for varying periods of time to earn a greater range of credentials, we need a financial aid system to support that model. Not an easy task for the office of Federal Student Aid (FSA). This massive, complex arm of the Education Department uses antiquated mainframes to dispense more than $120 billion in financial aid each year, overseeing more than $1.7 trillion in loans from the 42.9 million recipients with outstanding student loan debt. If it were a bank, FSA would be among the largest in the world, with holdings that exceed that of Barclays, Goldman Sachs, and Deutsche Bank.[2] Rethinking federal financial aid means starting with the basic flaw: time.

EQUITY AND FEDERAL POLICY

First, a little history. The Higher Education Act of 1965 (HEA) was signed into law by President Lyndon Johnson as part of his administration's War on Poverty. It was designed to help low-income students attend college, making the federal government the largest funder of financial aid for a college education, with states, banks, and suppliers of scholarships being the others. The law was relatively straightforward, administering funds directly to colleges through the Educational Opportunity Grant (EOG) program as outlined in Title IV of the act. In the following decades, the financial aid system was expanded, programs were added, middle-class families were included, loan repayment options proliferated, and eligibility came to cover part-time as well as full-time programs. Like some of the old farmhouses that dot the landscape of New England (my home region), where outbuildings and additions were built in haphazard fashion and without an overall plan, the federal financial aid system is a hodge-podge of programs, difficult to administer, baffling for students and families, and wedded to its inadequate, time-based understanding of learning. Like those old farmhouses, with their drafty windows, inefficient heating systems, and labyrinthine passageways, the law is not well suited for how we currently live and learn—even less so amid the wave of changes to higher education that the pandemic has accelerated.

The Higher Education Act is meant to be revisited, revised, and reauthorized every four to five years. But as with all major policy making in our era, the reworking of our higher education policy is hotly contested territory. It takes much longer to reach agreement, with the last HEA reauthorization happening in 2008, ten years after the previous extension of the original 1965 act. With Democrats in the White House and just barely controlling both chambers of the US Congress, there might be hope for an overdue reauthorization of HEA in the first two years of the Biden administration. However, a long list of contentious issues must be resolved for that to happen, including the regulation of for-profit colleges, the balancing of consumer protection versus innovation, Title IX and the proper rights of victims of sexual assault and those accused (and the role of institutions in managing those cases), the role and efficacy of accreditors, and proposals for free college and loan forgiveness.

Not everything about the HEA is contentious, however. There seems to be bipartisan support for simplification and streamlining, such as reducing the number of loan repayment programs from ten to one (or at least only a few), and more transparency and reporting of data covering both institutional and program levels. Likewise, after years of prodding by Senator Lamar Alexander, the retired Tennessee Republican and former university president who chaired the Senate's education committee until 2021, a federal spending bill enacted late in 2020 finally simplified the Free Application for Federal Student Aid (FAFSA) form.[3] The infamously complicated FAFSA now will feature about 36 questions rather than the 108 it had long featured (triple the length of a standard income tax form).

The complexity of the system and even forms like the FAFSA deeply disadvantage low-income students who tend to lack the support and guidance to navigate the system. As Bill Gates points out:

[T]he overly complex and confusing financial aid system is failing the students most in need of assistance, preventing them from pursuing their dreams of attending college.

Only about half of low-income high school seniors who would qualify for federal student loans or grants apply for them. And just under one-third of low-income high school seniors who would be eligible for Pell Grants, a federal subsidy for the neediest students that does not need to be paid back, take advantage of them when they start college. Without financial aid, many students drop out of school or decide not to go to college at all.[4]

The financial aid system—born out of legislation that sought to make college a reality for low-income students and to reinforce American higher education as an engine of social mobility—now gets in their way.

The need to correct these injustices is urgent. Huge numbers of lower-income students have left the education pipeline during the pandemic, with experts fearing many will never return. High schools where at least 40 percent of students are low income have seen an alarming 18.5-percent drop in FAFSA completions.[5] Overall US enrollment at community colleges was down 10 percent in the fall of 2020, according to the National Student Clearinghouse Research Center, with a 21-percent decrease in enrollments of first-year students—and a nearly 30-percent drop among Black, Latino, and Native American first-year students.[6] Even scarier, the worst may be yet to come for this COVID-19 cohort. Community colleges saw a whopping 37-percent decline in fall enrollments of students who graduated from low-income high schools in 2020.[7] Overall college enrollment for low-income high school graduates was down by 29 percent. This declining enrollment is a catastrophe that could help keep millions of people in poverty.

The pandemic has been an extraordinary "collision of crises" that further exposed already yawning inequities and inequalities, according to Richard V. Reeves, a writer and senior fellow at the Brookings Institution. "The whole U.S. economy was like a giant pre-existing condition," Reeves said in June 2020.[8] "And COVID came along and exposed it all." Black, Latino, and other underserved student groups and their families have been the hardest hit during the pandemic. And not surprisingly, given the impossible demands many lower-income Americans are facing, time is one of the top barriers people cite in considering whether to pursue more education. Fully half of American adults surveyed in a poll conducted in late 2020 said balancing college with other responsibilities would be a challenge, slightly less than the 59 percent who cited cost, the top concern.[9] If our financial aid system remains based on time, reflecting the industry's reliance on the credit hour, it will be difficult to develop new models that can work far better for underserved learners for whom time and funding are precisely the problems.

Competency-based education is the rare innovation to have champions on both sides of the aisle in the US Congress, including influential education committee members. The reauthorization of the Higher Education Act offers the best opportunity to support education models based on actual learning and not time. If reauthorization remains elusive (remember, it usually takes years to negotiate), any stimulus bills Congress creates to counter the ongoing economic havoc wreaked by the pandemic offer another opportunity to attach a demonstration project to new legislation at a time when bold solutions are being sought. Either way, this is not an argument for dramatically dropping the credit hour and radically revamping higher education overnight. That kind of sudden disruption of an industry—what happened in journalism or the music industry, which were upended in a seeming heartbeat—does not happen in heavily regulated industries with enormous sums of public money at stake. As with health care, which in many ways resembles higher education, change comes slowly.

Also, while the credit hour system is really bad at measuring actual learning and not well suited for student-centered program design (especially for the poor), the industry is built around this standard, the FSA knows how to administer it, and consumer protection advocates believe it offers some level of protection for students. While it may not be the federal government's fault for using the credit hour as a basis for our financial aid system—it could only work with what higher education provided—it has built an enormous and complex system that only knows how to do this time-based method. If we are to shift away from time to actual student learning as a basis for our higher education system, we will need the financial aid system to make a commensurate shift.

Salt Lake Community College used a federal grant during the Obama administration to create noncredit, competency-based programs in high-demand fields. As the project was getting off the ground, administrators at the two-year college realized they would need to prevent students from completing competencies too quickly so that they wouldn't have to pay back federal aid they received. Our time-based financial aid system actually penalizes accelerated learning. "We just wouldn't even let our students get into that situation. They would be counseled that if you fin-ish early, you will have to pay back Uncle Sam. And he will come calling," says Eric Heiser, the former dean at the college who helped design the pro-gram. "We're trying to get these people in, out, and into a better-paying job and yet we tie both their hands behind their back and then they have to lift one leg and jump around."

What policy makers should consider is a genuine non-credit-hour alternative for the awarding of financial aid. Let those institutions and pro-grams wed to the credit hour continue to operate as they do, though, one hopes, with long-needed updates to the current system. However, along-side the ongoing credit-hour system, colleges and universities should be able to choose an outcomes- or competency-based option for disbursing federal financial aid to eligible students in such programs. (Non-college providers offering high-quality college-level learning should be allowed access to federal financial aid for their students, as I will argue later.) Such a parallel track would use competency instead of the credit hour as the basic building block for aid calculations. But it could retain the current system's eligibility requirements and aid limits.

Take the University of Michigan, for example. Most of the flagship pub-lic university's vast operations could continue to rely on the credit-hour standard. But some components could try the competency-based aid option. Michigan's Medical School, for example, includes some programs that would be well suited for this new framework. Any institution that wants to be included in the demonstration project would have great free-dom in how it delivers the program but would have to show how it adheres to the kinds of frameworks outlined in previous chapters on competencies and assessment. An audit using something like the Competency-Based Education Network's Quality Assurance Review could be easily adopted.[10]

The next section will outline what financial aid for competency-based education might look like. The devil is always in the details, however, and the federal financial aid system is bedeviled like few others. So a more detailed version of what is broadly outlined here, for policy wonks and others who want to go deeper, is included on this book's accompany-ing website.

Federal financial aid is only one leg of a three-legged regulatory stool often called "The Triad." The other two legs are accreditation, which is focused on quality, and state authorization, which often provides some measure of consumer protection while affirming an institution's legal right to operate. A competency-based pathway has implications for those areas as well, which I will address in this chapter's final two sections.

A BETTER WAY FORWARD

Building a financial aid system for competency-based education begins with the following assumptions:

- The federal government will continue to set limits on what it's willing to make available to students. Today, under the credit hour, a lifetime limit determines how much grant money students can receive, as well as how much in federal student loans they can borrow. The current amounts are
  - $38,070 for Pell Grants (generally a $6,345 annual amount over six years if a student is eligible for the maximum award)
  - $57,500 in federal loans for undergraduate education
  - $138,500 in federal loans for graduate education
- Our proposed system assumes students in this degree pathway would have the equivalent access and limits as students in the incumbent credit-hour system.
- The credit hour is not only a measure of time; it also seeks to provide a measure of weight. That is, beyond a measure of time, the credit hour also tries to define how much learning takes place (think topic coverage, rigor, and depth instead of time). However imperfect and ill defined that measure may be, our model assumes that one competency equals one credit hour in terms of weight, what we call the 1C:1C exchange rate at SNHU. For example, completion of six competencies would be equivalent to the knowledge and skills in two

courses of three credits each—no matter how quickly or slowly a student mastered them.

- Time will not matter, so aid can be dispersed at any rate over any time. But aid should be aligned with how much learning is undertaken using the 1C:1C measure of weight. In that sense, the student can draw down from their total fixed amount of aid on the basis of how much learning they are attempting, not how long they are learning.
- The system does not address quality, which is left to a well-designed accreditation process.

With those assumptions in mind, the total amount of aid available would be drawn down by a student on an apportioned cost per competency (amounts are rounded up and down as appropriate). A student with maximum Pell Grant and federal loan eligibility would have $95,070 to draw down. (New legislative limits on Pell Grants and loans can be factored into a student's calculation as Congress makes adjustments.) Most undergraduate bachelor's degree programs require students to complete 120 credit hours. So, using the 1C:1C exchange rate, each competency at the undergraduate level would yield $792.25 of available aid ($95,070 divided by 120).

A note on the 1C:1C equivalency. Many smart proponents of competency-based education would rightly argue that competencies come in different "sizes." Some are more complex and take longer to master, whereas others may be important but take much less time. As a result, they say a rigid one-competency-to-one-credit equivalency is too constraining. The issue here is that if we think of a competency as a new measure of weight—some amount of knowledge and skills—it must be anchored to something. When the euro was introduced, a new measure of monetary value, it had to be anchored to the dollar for anyone to understand its weight or value. In similar fashion, at least for some time, anchoring competencies to the credit hour as a measure of weight, not time, is likely necessary to prevent abuses by bad actors that collect too much aid for too little learning, an important safeguard if consumer-protection-minded regulators are to support our proposal.

Back to the model. Imagine an undergraduate student—Martha, we'll call her—whose financial circumstances make her eligible for the full federal Pell Grant and student loan amounts. She has the lifetime pool of $95,070 available for her education. Martha enrolls in a competency-based associate degree program in accounting, which consists of sixty competencies for which she must demonstrate mastery to complete. That means Martha has up to $47,535 of federal financial aid (Pell Grants and loans) available to her for the sixty competencies and completion of her associate degree, no matter how fast or slow she progresses through the program. That leaves her the same amount for any further education she then pursues, such as completion of her bachelor's degree.

How would those funds be paid out? First, a bit of explanation: the federal government makes available aid calculations based on what it describes as the "total cost of attendance," a combination of what the federal financial aid system calls "direct costs" (tuition and books) and indirect costs (housing, transportation, loan fees, childcare, and other expenses). The FSA sends all aid to the institution, which takes its portion out first and then sends the remainder to the student as a "refund" to help cover indirect expenses. If the institutional portion in each semester is $15,000 and the eligible aid comes in at $18,000 (because the total cost of attendance allows it), the additional $3,000 goes to the student to help cover indirect expenses while being a student.

In my proposed model, Martha can be enrolled in up to fifteen competencies at a time, which means that no more than $11,880 of federal aid can be drawn down at any one time. For the sake of simplicity, let's assume that the college pegs its total cost of attendance to the per-competency limit of $792. From that $11,880, the institution would take its tuition and fees, and Martha would get the balance paid to her to help cover other costs she has as a student. If Martha's college charges $650 per competency in this example, the $142 balance goes to her as part of Martha's total cost of attendance.

Currently, the underlying philosophy around aid is that it is earned each day the student is in attendance, but the funds are entirely paid out on the front end. So, if a student starts a program and then drops out, the college and the student must return to the federal government a portion of the aid collected up front in a process called R2T4 (for "Return To Title IV"), based on how many days the student was enrolled before dropping out. The college uses R2T4 to pay back its portion and the student's portion, and then has to collect the student portion from the student. Students typically are not aware of this view of earned aid and tend to be understandably cranky to get a bill for the aid that was returned to the federal government on their behalf.

By tying aid to competencies, my system would go a long way toward ensuring that taxpayers support actual learning, not how long someone attended classes that were ill informed by inflated grades based on poor assessment practices. But to fully dismantle the worst flaws of the time-based status quo, the federal government should distribute 50 percent of the eligible aid amount when a student enrolls in a competency and then allocate the other half at the successful completion of the competency. Unlike in the current system, the institution gets no more than 50 percent of its tuition up front. This approach incentivizes the institution to stay focused on student success and ensuring that low-income students get support for their indirect costs and are not forced to wait until the second 50 percent is allocated from the federal financial aid system, an important detail in terms of equity.

No more than fifteen competencies could be covered by aid at any given time. And as competencies are completed, new ones could be started on a rolling basis. That frees up additional aid (again, based on our maximum limit of $792 per competency, never exceeding fifteen at a time). Capping the number of competencies covered by aid would prevent an unscrupulous provider from enrolling new students in a large number of competencies, collecting a great deal of money up front, and then not worrying about students actually completing—a version of the abuses we have seen with some large, for-profit online providers.

SHORT-TERM ALTERNATIVES

Let's return to Martha. She enrolls in her first fifteen competencies, and her college gets its 50 percent of the $9,750 it charges for fifteen competencies ($650 times 15). Martha gets 50 percent of the $2,130 she will receive for this amount of learning ($142 times 15). At the completion of each competency, the college and Martha get the other half they are owed, and Martha can start a new competency, drawing down additional aid. Time is irrelevant here, but pace is rewarded. If Martha masters ten competencies in just a month, she will earn $1,420, and her college will receive its full $6,500 in just four weeks. If Martha struggles with those last five competencies and takes twelve months to complete them, neither she nor her college will see the second half of the aid for those five competencies. Martha and her college have an incentive to bear down on barriers to her completion of the competencies. And she can still move as quickly as she can through others, starting new competencies and the additional aid that comes with them. Yes, an unscrupulous college could make it easy for her to complete competencies. But that's where rigorous quality control comes in, as we'll see in the next section. Remember, federal financial aid is not about quality assurance (even though consumer protection advocates try to leverage it that way). And we're talking about a better way to disperse aid in an outcomes-based system.

This approach promises several other advantages.

- It distributes and limits risk by paying for success, not time served. The Education Department would pay 50 percent up front with a cap on the total number of competencies, while the institution and the student must complete a competency to see the 50 percent they are due.
- Time-related standards under current aid dispersal rules (satisfactory academic progress, term and academic year, minimum weeks of instruction) all go away. The equation becomes simplified to how many competencies the student enrolls in (up to fifteen) and how many they complete.

- Prior learning assessment is legitimized and rewarded. It is not eligible for aid today. And FSA's worry about not paying for learning that happened before (already somewhat illogical) is no longer an issue, because the "when," a time-based notion, gives way to claims and assessments around demonstrated learning.
- There is greater incentive for program completion for everyone involved. Right now, almost half of students who start degree programs never complete. Because success is rewarded, institutions will direct more resources to students who need the most help.

The system also is better suited to the rapid increase in the shorter term, nondegree programs described in chapter 2. As a recent survey found:

Amidst a global pandemic, American teenagers remain steadfast in their belief that higher education plays a key role in their future success; however, the paths they are planning to take after high school differ from previous generations. In fact, more than half are open to something other than a four-year degree and 70 percent want to follow their own educational path.[11]

Surveys conducted during the pandemic have found a consistent preference for nondegree, skills-based credentials among American workers who are interested in pursuing more education.[12] The top reasons they cite for preferring these programs are value, a better fit for their lives and needs, and relevance to job and careers. For low-income learners, the deferred payoff of a two- or four-year degree often feels like a luxury of time they cannot afford. And many want programs of shorter length that are laser focused on high-demand skills that will help them get a job.

Congress currently is mulling whether to extend eligibility for Pell Grants to shorter-term nondegree programs. Students currently can receive federal need-based aid for programs lasting as little as fifteen weeks. But bipartisan proposals in Congress would open up aid to programs as short as eight weeks, including ones that are noncredit.[13] The predictable battle lines are forming, with consumer advocates pushing back on what they worry will be a race to the bottom to siphon away Pell money for worthless credentials offered by unscrupulous providers. They need only to point to massive failures of previous short-term programs to make their case.[14] Meanwhile, business groups and community colleges back the push for so-called short-term Pell, saying it would help workers who have lost jobs and wages during the pandemic gain skills to get back to work. Ideally, these short-term programs also would stack up to a degree as students return to higher education later in their career.

Everything we know about work today suggests that individuals will need to go in and out of a learning ecosystem across the span of ever-longer careers.[15] Even if you do not move jobs, your job will evolve, changing out from under you, and you will need to retool. The pace of change is rapid, and learning can no longer be relegated to two or four years when we are straight out of high school, then neglected as we happily move through our careers. Technical skills often have a half-life of fewer than three years. People will need shorter-term learning options to stay current and competitive—just the right amount of additional learning in just the right way at just the right time. That could mean two months or two weeks or even two days. If we do not provide for some shorter-term sub-degree programs in our federal financial aid system, we will once again replicate inequities that deprive low-income Americans of the educational tools they need to thrive. However, the financial aid approach I propose reflects our new reality by viewing aid as a *pool of money* that can be used over a lifetime, with returning students drawing down aid for educational upskilling whenever they need it. If we think of that pool as a lifelong learning account (which means dropping the rule that Pell can't be used for post-baccalaureate or short-term programs), exciting possibilities open up. For example:

- We could create programs that incentivize both employers and employees to add more funds into life-long learning accounts.
- Those accounts could be portable, staying with the person throughout their career and giving them more career mobility.

- Students would have incentive to seek out more affordable under-graduate programs, preserving more of their total lifetime pool of financial aid dollars for more eventual education.

REALIZING LIFELONG LEARNING

Policy makers also could cap available dollars for study that leads to a bachelor's degree at 80 percent of the lifetime limit, preserving 20 percent of the funding for later use in shorter-term education programs, the kind everyone will need and that the industry already is seeing with innovative new forms of online graduate degrees and certificates.

Other pools of federal money could be used to further support short-term training programs, such as the Labor Department's Workforce Innovation and Opportunity Act (WIOA) funding, which supports training for displaced adults, opportunity youth, and job attainment. Jamie Merisotis, who leads the Lumina Foundation and is one of our better thinkers around workforce development, argues that the Departments of Education and Labor should be merged into one Department of Talent, reflecting the integral relationship of K–12, postsecondary education, and the workforce. (See *America Needs Talent*, his 2015 book).[16] The federal financial aid system can be one part of a more cohesive talent strategy, supporting degrees and shorter-term programs (which it does now), as long as the latter have strong, demonstrable outcomes for in-demand skills that make a difference in students' lives. A smart federal strategy would complement that funding with a lifelong source of additional support, recognizing that everyone now needs periodic upskilling.

The idea of a lifetime pool of dollars for continuous learning is not new. More than twenty years ago the Council for Adult and Experiential Learning (CAEL) created the concept of Lifelong Learning Accounts (LiLAs). The idea is to create a fund from which adult learners can draw down support for ongoing learning across their careers. In 2001, with support from the Ford Foundation, CAEL launched a demonstration project in Chicago that focused on low-income workers, many of whom had more than one job. An independent evaluation of the program in 2006 was very encouraging.[17] The results included

- high participation rates among workers who were willing to invest in themselves and to add to their LiLA accounts, despite having precious little extra income to spare
- high levels of use of the accounts for the intended purpose, with employees taking courses and programs that were "somewhat relevant" to their current jobs and "very relevant" to the work to which they aspired
- almost half of the employees involved reporting that the program prompted them to go back to school
- employer satisfaction with the program, including a greater appreciation for education in the workplace with some employers even expanding their support for education beyond the program

A handful of states and cities have gone on to experiment with lifelong learning accounts, and countries like France and Singapore have adopted them.[18] The Brookings Institution has proposed a model that projects twenty-three million Americans contributing to their own accounts over ten years.[19]

LiLAs always were conceived as *additions* to the financial aid system that currently helps learners pay for college. My proposal expands the LiLA concept to reframe federal financial aid programs—which already include lifetime limits, essentially offering to eligible students a pool of dollars from which to draw—as lifelong learning accounts themselves, ones that feature the possibility of adding to and replenishing that pool from contributions outside of the federal financial aid systems. These contributions could be through foundations, for example, or other third-party entities that might target support for a population, geography, or industry, as well as through employee and employer contributions. We would then have a financial aid system built for today—serving learners of all ages, across the span of their lives, supporting a broader array of educational options, paying for actual demonstrated learning—that would be more equitable and flexible than our outdated system and far easier for students to navigate.

This new model for federal aid can help ensure that short-term credentials and other alternatives to traditional degree programs work for students and taxpayers. Of course, those learning paths and programs must adhere to the high standards of competency-based education, confirmed through accreditation, with the transparency of college-level learning and rigorous assessment that comes with it. Previous attempts at regulating short-term programs used time-based measures, including length of term, clock hours of supervised training, and numbers of credit-hour equivalencies. These efforts were not effective at curbing abuse because they looked at inputs that can be easily manipulated, unlike measurable outcomes. And none of the measures included risk sharing by the provider or built-in aid limits. More on that in a moment. As a result, the history of short-term programs is mixed at best.[20] Sometimes these credentials open a basic entryway to full-time work, but too often the path of short-term educational programs fails to lead beyond low-income jobs. We need good shorter-term programs, and low-income students will need help accessing them through financial aid. But these programs must be far better than what is available in the market today.

A competency-based approach to shorter-term college-level programs, with rigorous assessment and demonstrated outcomes, can address both the *efficacy* of shorter-term programs and the *need* for a learning ecosystem in which degrees remain primary milestones, but where a greater variety of sub-degree credentials precede and follow degree attainment and fit in a more coherent framework than is provided by the current and incoherent mix of shorter-term programs.

An educational system freed from time and supported with a commensurate system of awarding financial aid would face several hurdles, with institutional inertia being perhaps the highest one to clear. With all the accumulated processes around a credit-hour basis for learning and financial aid, higher education simply is unprepared to make such a shift. With students progressing at whatever pace makes sense for them, it will be hard for institutions to plan on resource allocation. What happens if everyone slows down and instructors are left sitting around waiting for projects to be completed and assessed? What if there is a surge of completions? Time-based systems, with their fixed calendars, set term structures and relatively predictable enrollments. As a result, they are much easier to administer. The Education Department has no experience, processes, or systems in place to support this new model. And it has a responsibility to carefully steward billions of dollars. Consumer protection advocates remain leery of broadening federal support for competency-based education without a better understanding of how to ensure quality. This is why keeping that system intact but offering the *voluntary option* of this new model allows for the increasing number of institutions that are doing competency-based education to put up their hands and sort out what is required, rather than asking a large, entrenched system to reform itself or change practices. We could then get to watch a competency-based system grow and flourish alongside the incumbent system, allowing us to compare its efficacy and giving students a choice.

A headlong rush to create a competency-based education option for dispersing federal financial aid shouldn't (and won't) happen. But administrative convenience also should not prevent experimentation with models of higher education that could work better for students we currently are failing to serve. Convenience is no defense of inequity. Congress can authorize a *demonstration project* to test drive a new system, inviting institutions and other necessary stakeholders to volunteer to try it. Legislation for a demonstration project would task the Secretary of Education's office with selecting which institutions can participate. The Secretary also would be responsible for waiving certain financial aid regulations and statutes to test the competency-based approach to aid disbursement, and to strictly monitor the demonstration as it progresses. Demonstrations are designed as learning labs, a controlled innovation sandbox in which we try new approaches and carefully track our results, eventually enabling the broader adoption of innovations and policies that work—for students, providers, and taxpayers.

This form of testing innovation within the confines of well-designed guardrails would allow us to get the system right, realize the simplicity that has long been sought, and implement a modern technology infrastructure that might eventually replace the antiquated one that now supports our federal financial aid system. All while carefully controlling risk and managing the bad actors that always are attracted to the federal trough.

THE REGULATORY TRIAD

Accreditation is the leg of the higher education Triad tasked with overseeing institutional quality.[21] Three different types of accreditors, all nongovernmental agencies, do this work:

- six regional accrediting agencies, each covering a specified region of the country, which accredit colleges and universities, but not specific programs offered by those institutions
- national accreditors, which also accredit institutions and often have a specific area of focus, such as continuing education and training
- specialized or programmatic accreditors that look only at a specific field, such as nursing, engineering, and business

Regional and national accreditors are gatekeepers to aid. No college or university can receive federal financial aid for its students unless the institution is first accredited by one of these agencies. (The Education Department recognizes sixty-two gatekeeper accreditors). For decades, accreditation was little noticed outside of higher education circles. It sets minimum *thresholds* for quality and uses peer review to support ongoing quality improvement—that is, teams of faculty and staff from various peer institutions conduct the review of any given member institution slated for accreditation review. Accreditation historically focused on an institution's stated mission and how well it delivered on that promise, looking especially at academics, the role of faculty, and general care of students. Effective management was addressed in standards around governance, planning, finance, and disclosure, but with a lighter touch. Overall, accreditation was based much more on inputs than outcomes. That reflects the approach to academic quality the industry has generally taken, which is in essence a faith-based system. If an institution had the right *inputs*—enough faculty members with PhDs, systems of governance (especially around academics), appropriate offices and functions to support students, and even, for a long time, enough books in the library—we had faith in its outputs of students and the quality of their education. Accreditors were patient as well. Struggling institutions could limp along for years, with their peer reviewers offering helpful counsel. Only in the rarest of cases was accreditation removed, in part because that sanction would cut off the flow of federal aid, a death sentence for the vast majority of colleges. The oversight process was considered a mostly private matter, and accreditors typically did not make their reviews and reports available to the public.

Everything has changed. In recent years accrediting agencies have taken fire from all sides:

- Advocates for innovation accuse the agencies of being too slow, too traditional, and of stifling improvements they want to see in program design and delivery.
- Consumer protection advocates cite lax oversight of bad players that offer low-quality programs and often take advantage of students. In some cases accreditation has even been awarded to fraudulent enterprises.
- During the Obama era, the administration and many other critics viewed accreditors as lacking in their oversight of for-profit institutions. But the Trump administration accused the agencies of unfair and onerous handling of for-profits.
- Students, often burdened with debt and frustrated with their career prospects (especially after the Great Recession), have held accreditors at fault for their predicament.

A persistent criticism of accreditors is that they lack the fortitude or ability (or both) to crack down on bad actors, particularly institutions that can fight sanctions with the threat of lawsuits and political pressure. Critics of accreditation argue that the agencies have been downright lax, pointing out that some of the worst abusers of the federal financial aid system, later shut down by the Department of Education, were all accredited and in good standing—a stark signal of failure in their eyes.

For example, Sylvia Manning, the president of the Higher Learning Commission (HLC), the largest of the regional accreditors, was grilled during a hearing held in 2011 by then-Senator Tom Harkin, the Iowa Democrat who led the education committee.[22] He questioned whether accreditors were equipped to oversee multistate corporations that operated for-profit college chains. And Harkin accused the commission and other accreditors of being soft on low-quality for-profits, including one he called an "absolute scam." A couple years later, HLC effectively shut down Ivy Bridge College, a for-profit that offered online, two-year degrees through an innovative partnership with Tiffin University, a small non-profit institution located in Ohio. Many thought the Higher Learning Commission was looking for a target after getting torched by Senate Democrats. And Ivy Bridge was a softer one than the big for-profit chains. The company went belly up and later sued the accreditor.[23]

City College of San Francisco's long-running accreditation saga was an example of how public colleges can also push back hard on their accreditor overseers.[24] The large community college has long wrestled with big deficits, and it faced bankruptcy in 2012. A state audit found that the college's payroll for faculty and staff members accounted for 92 percent of its expenditures. And only thirty-nine administrators were trying to run the college, which enrolled ninety thousand students. The Accrediting Commission for Community and Junior Colleges, City College's regional accreditor, found that student services at the college were lacking, buildings were falling apart, and it was not adequately tracking student outcomes. The college also was operating with three days' worth of cash reserves.

The commission decided to yank City College's approval in 2013. A long, politically charged fight ensued, featuring a lawsuit filed by San Francisco's city attorney against the accreditor. US Representative Nancy Pelosi got involved, joining other members of Congress in condemning the accreditor for a "failure of leadership" on the City College crisis, stressing the harm that would be done to students if City College were to go out of business.[25] In the end, the college beat back the sanction, and the accreditor faced its own multiyear fight for survival.[26] Whether or not the commission was in the right, the fracas showed accreditors struggle to crack down when they find problems, particularly with politically connected public colleges or deep-pocketed for-profit institutions. And oversight isn't complete without the nuclear option of dropping approval and access to federal aid. Meanwhile, City College continues to have a hard time balancing its budget.[27]

More generally, accreditors face pressure to be more rigorous in their assessments of quality, to put more weight on student outcomes, and to act faster and more transparently when they identify issues. Accreditation standards have been revised to bring more attention to outcomes, effectiveness, and measurements of efficacy. But so far at least, that scrutiny has not led to meaningful improvements in accreditors' oversight of low-quality programs, and consumer advocates remain largely dismissive of accreditors' effectiveness in ensuring quality and protecting against bad actors in the industry.

The agencies have entered an era of "new normal accreditation," according to Susan Phillips and Kevin Kinser, coauthors of the 2018 book, *Accreditation on the Edge*. As they write:

> *The new normal's role is, first and foremost, a compliance and information sharing or transparency one, above all, assuring and making public an institution's minimum performance in serving students. Expectations and standards for the new-normal role are increasingly set not by accreditors but by government, especially at the federal level, influenced by students, the public, and media. Accreditation, once viewed as an arcane and boring undertaking, essentially invisible outside of higher education, has become public property.*[28]

In 2015, Arne Duncan, then the US Education Secretary, called accreditors "watchdogs that don't bite." Duncan pressured the agencies to be more transparent about standards for accreditation and the formal actions they took in dealing with institutions. The National Advisory Committee on Institutional Quality and Integrity (NACIQI) is a bipartisan advisory committee that periodically reviews accreditors and makes recommendations to the Education Department. I'm a member of the committee, appointed by Senator Patty Murray, the Washington Democrat who now chairs the Senate's education committee. When I was nominated, a friend and former White House official asked me why I'd want to be part of such a bureaucratic and boring entity. It has been anything but that, as the battle over the proper role of accreditors has raged in each of NACIQI's two annual meetings.

For example, in a 2016 meeting, the American Bar Association (ABA), which is the accrediting agency for law schools, came before the committee for its periodic review. The Education Department's staff review cited some minor documentation issues, and the ABA team expected routine approval of their ongoing status as accreditor of law schools. Instead, the ABA's representatives were taken to task on student outcomes and why the agency tolerated law schools with low bar exam passage rates that were saddling their graduates with enormous debt and little prospect of a law career. I was among those who voted to recommend the removal of the ABA's recognition, which would remove them as accreditors of law schools. The committee went through three rounds of split voting before it landed on a recommendation to renew recognition for only one year. The Education Department subsequently ignored NACIQI's recommendation, as it sometimes does.

In that same meeting, we recommended the removal of recognition for the Accrediting Council for Independent Colleges and Schools (ACICS), the large national accreditor, which accredited hundreds of for-profit institutions, many of them engaged in fraudulent practices and systematic misleading of students. It was a dramatic, even unprecedented move by the committee. While the Education Department accepted our recommendation and removed ACICS's recognition, Betsy DeVos, the Trump administration's Education Secretary and a defender of for-profit education, reinstated the agency in 2018. The Biden administration then reversed that decision during its first month.[29] Despite the back and forth, the trend here is that accreditors in their quality-assurance role increasingly are being forced to look at outcomes. As Phillips and Kinser write, a "process that was once solely about meeting standards focused on academic concerns such as faculty and curriculum is now, at least in part, built around what government thinks is important, for example, nonacademic issues such as the cost of education, student debt, loan repayment and default rates, and results of licensure examinations."[30] In other words, outcomes. As we saw in chapter 4, the outcomes movement has been problematic and only marginally effective (its critics would be harsher). But it paves the way for competency-based education's powerful coupling of greater freedom in program design *and* more accountability.

This combination of freedom in design and rigor in assessment is part of why a competency-based model is so timely and lends itself to more effective methods of quality assurance. The EQUIP Program mentioned in chapter 2 was meant to encourage more competency-based programs and to bring new providers into the Title IV ecosystem (which earned it plenty of resistance from consumer protection advocates within the Education Department, eventually spelling its demise). But it also sought to encourage new approaches to quality assurance, to potentially inform improvements to the accreditation process, and even to lead to the eventual establishment of a new class of outcomes-focused accreditors. The 2015 notice for the experiment in the *Federal Register* included this passage:

Outputs, Which, Where Applicable, Must Be Disaggregated to Show Outcomes Specifically for Low-Income Students

1. *How are students performing on program assessments?*
2. *How are students progressing through the program? For example:*
   - *Retention rate?*
   - *Withdrawal rate?*
   - *Average time to completion?*
   - *Completion rate (within 100 percent and 150 percent of expected time)?*
3. *What are the actual program outcomes for students (e.g., entry into subsequent phase of study, career, etc.)? For example:*

Employment outcomes, for all programs that have a stated mission focused on employment (include method for how these outcomes are measured):
- *Job placement rates in field of study?*
- *Average length of time between completion of program and employment in field of study?*
- *Job retention rates?*
- *Median starting salaries?*
- *Transfer rates to other academic or vocational programs, where applicable.*
- *Certifications and licensure exam passage rates, where applicable.*

4. *What are the following ratios for the program, where relevant?*
- *Published tuition and fees versus earnings.*
- *Average net price versus earnings.*
- *Median student debt versus earnings.*

5. *How does the program rate on measures of student satisfaction? For example, how does the program rate in the following:*
- *Comments from students about what made them successful or unsuccessful in the program?*
- *A rigorous and transparent methodology for gathering and synthesizing customer satisfaction measures?*

With a focus on outcomes and a demand for clarity on the claims a program makes for its graduates and about the rigor in its assessments, quality assurance moves from its faith-based approach to one based on transparency, good design, rigor in assessment, and demonstrated outcomes. It's responsive to the new normal in accreditation.

Most importantly, a focus on transparency in claims made for learning, strong assessment practices, and measurable outputs reframes the tired consumer-protection-versus-innovation debate in policy making on postsecondary education. Too often, consumer protection advocates look at anything new as an invitation for unscrupulous players to cheat the system under the guise of innovation (in their defense, it often has been).

Their approach is often prescriptive, saying what is and is not allowed in program design. The result inherently squelches genuine innovations, in part because policy should always *follow* practice and not try to anticipate it. Consumer protection advocates should embrace an alternative to our longstanding and challenged approach to accreditation. We can bring transparency and rigor around the three main questions posed by an outcomes-based quality-assurance process:

- What claims do you make for what your students know and can do with that knowledge?
- How do you assess them?
- What are their outcomes?

When we are satisfied with the answers to these key questions, we can invite as much innovation as possible. This approach to accreditation and quality-assurance would then align with our proposed model for outcomes-based financial aid, allowing the federal government to play its role as funder and accreditors to play a more rigorous role around quality. Both would be more effective. And the disharmony that exists today in the relationship would dissipate, at least for the outcomes-based programs they would support.

What then the role of the states, the third player in the Triad? If part of the goal here is to return each Triad member to its originally intended role, the states should focus on licensure, compliance with state laws governing businesses and their operations, and consumer protections. On one level, that function is no different than it is for any business that seeks to be incorporated in a state and subsequently is subject to the state's laws for operation. Every legal for-profit and nonprofit organization must be incorporated in a state if it wishes to operate there. Generally, states expect to license any college or university that has on-the-ground components of their program within their borders. State agencies then provide consumer protections to students, ranging from handling student complaints to preserving their records should their college or university go out of business. In 2018 the sudden and unexpected closure of a small Massachusetts institution, Mount Ida College, left state officials scrambling to manage the transition, support students, and put in place new legislation that seeks to ensure an early warning of financial distress among colleges, as well as processes for closure.[31] The profound impact on institutional finances during the pandemic has given greater weight to the states' role in protecting students who are deeply disadvantaged when their institutions suddenly close.

The growth of online education has raised questions about the states' role in the Triad for universities that operate nationwide, like SNHU, enrolling students in every state, but with ground-based presences only in some states. While students in a given state might want to enroll in a fully online program, in the early days of online education that state might still require the institution to be licensed there despite a lack of a physical presence. At one point, the Obama administration required states to license all online providers that enrolled any of their residents. But they also allowed states to instead join consortiums that offered reciprocal recognition of state licensure. Today, the National Council for State Authorization Reciprocity Agreements (NC-SARA) includes forty-nine states, Puerto Rico, the District of Columbia, and the US Virgin Islands, with California being the only holdout.[32] This solution has been sensible for online education, with states voluntarily agreeing to follow a common approach to approval and oversight.

The outcomes-based approach to federal financial aid and accreditation I propose has no real implications for states, except to reassure them that learning is better measured and quality more easily assessed.

USING EXISTING TOOLS

It is hard to overstate the difficulty of overhauling the federal financial aid system, a task so monumental that many will shrug and dismiss the idea out of hand as impossible. Time, despite its flaws as a measure of learning, is baked into a vast government bureaucracy, into the business structures of an immense industry, and into our thinking. It is utterly unrealistic to think we can reach agreement on a new basis for learning and thus financial aid, accreditation, and state approvals all at once. Getting buy-in of thousands of colleges and universities would be equally impractical. The change advocated for here would be deeply disruptive, in the best Clayton Christensen sense of the term (especially with his focus on those not well served by an incumbent industry). It could change everything and improve the industry, but would also generate desperate resistance by those threatened by new models. While we cannot ask higher education and its regulatory machine to abandon overnight deeply enmeshed time-based measures of learning and supporting aid, we can ask it to provide space for experimentation, innovation, and models that pave the way for more widespread change in the future.

Such experiments, when done well, can work. Congress has tools, including the ability to create demonstration projects, that can fundamentally impact higher education. That's how online education took hold in this country. Newly passed amendments to the Higher Education Act in 1998 created a demonstration project that gave approved colleges a waiver on what was known as the "50-percent rule."[33] That rule was put in place in 1992 to curb widespread abuses in the correspondence school industry. It required institutions that were eligible for federal financial aid to provide at least 50 percent of their instruction *on the ground*, in brick-and-mortar settings, and not simply through the mail. Because federal aid is the lifeblood of postsecondary education, almost nine hundred for-profit colleges—many of them diploma mills—went out of business in the first few years after the rule went into effect. Shortly thereafter, though, the rapid growth of the Internet changed almost every aspect of society, including higher education. And the 50-percent rule, which was designed to curb the abuses of correspondence schools, effectively prohibited fully online degree programs.

The 1998 demonstration project included fifteen approved institutions, eventually adding another nine. The final group featured a mix of nonprofit and for-profit colleges and universities, including Marlboro College, the institution I headed from 1996 to 2003. Demonstration projects are meant to provide learning that can then inform subsequent policy changes. The project on the 50-percent rule showed without a doubt that high-quality online programs were *possible,* with no on-the-ground component. By 2006, the Bush administration was ready to make new policy. It eliminated the 50-percent rule after plenty of prompting from the for-profit sector and its friends in high places. Sally Stroup, a former lobbyist for the University of Phoenix, was then the Assistant Secretary of Education. And then-US Representative John Boehner, a strong ally of for-profits, had become House Majority Leader. It is important to outline the ways in which this demonstration project fell short, as they feed the worries of consumer protection advocates and are instructive for how we might better design a demonstration project for competency-based education.

The lifting of the 50-percent rule failed to include necessary accompanying changes in the regulatory and quality-assurance frameworks for fully online degree programs. It drove meteoric growth in online enrollments, mostly by for-profits which aggressively pursued that growth with the backing of deep-pocketed investors. When the University of Phoenix joined the demonstration project in 2002, it enrolled 107,000 students. Eight years later it was by far the largest university in the country, enrolling almost 500,000 students, and was driven by fully online programs and often unscrupulous behavior. Other for-profit providers recklessly pursued similar growth.[34] They recruited heavily in underserved and low-income communities, inflated job-placement claims, falsified student information, and obscured their true costs. As a result, while they educated 12 percent of all students by 2010 (just four years after the 50-percent rule was dropped), for-profits accounted for half of all student loan defaults. One Education Department investigation showed that 72 percent of their associate-degree holders were making less money than high school dropouts.[35]

Spurred on by investigative reporting by *60 Minutes* and the *New York Times,* for-profit colleges soon came under intense scrutiny. The Harkin-led Senate education committee released a scathing 2012 report on the sector, and the Obama administration introduced new rules, issued fines, and then denied eligibility for Title IV funds to for-profit giants like Corinthian Colleges and ITT Educational Services.[36] The resulting closures of those chains led to federal loan forgiveness for students who attended them (costing taxpayers hundreds of millions of dollars the companies will never repay) and put the for-profits into steep decline. The once-mighty University of Phoenix now enrolls fewer than ninety thousand students (though a pandemic surge in online enrollments may have halted or even reversed its downward enrollment trend for a while). Some large for-profits have morphed into education service providers, dropping their universities and degree programs then contracting with nonprofit colleges to remain in the online education market.[37] And some have converted to nonprofits themselves. The sector's long-time critics have fiercely opposed both types of arrangements. And the US Government Accountability Office in 2021 found that the Education Department failed to adequately scrutinize nonprofit conversions.[38]

Does that mean the demonstration project was a failure? Not at all. We learned that high-quality, fully online degree programs *can* work. While some for-profit participants in the project went on to become bad actors, nonprofits like Western Governors University, the University of Maryland University College (now University of Maryland Global Campus), the Connecticut Distance Learning Consortium, Regis University, and the Jesuit-NET Consortium did very good work after participating. WGU and UMGC now educate tens of thousands of students in well-designed, rigorous, high-value degree programs that are entirely virtual. We also learned that for a great many students, fully online programs simply work better than traditionally delivered ones tethered to place and time. Students who were working, taking care of family, suffering limited access to the kinds of programs they wanted, or grappling with unreliable schedules found the flexibility and convenience they needed in fully online programs. The demonstration project is not to blame for what came afterward: elimination of the 50-percent rule without commensurate safeguards and quality-assurance frameworks, the nonprofit sector mostly looking down its nose at online education and thus ceding that market to for-profits, and the frequent misalignment of shareholder value with mission-based care of students. The demonstration project taught us what good-quality online education can look like. Today the nonprofit sector has reclaimed the online education market, and it is a rare college or university that does not offer online programs (especially after the pandemic forced everyone to give a try, even if grudgingly so). That original demonstration project transformed higher education and brought it into the digital age.

Congress needs to authorize a demonstration project for competency-based and other forms of learning not bound by time. It should have three goals:

- to learn from competency-based education programs included in the project and to understand what a genuinely outcomes-based model requires
- to design the financial aid awarding methodologies and necessary systems required to align with and support these new models
- to find and encourage new forms of quality assurance that are appropriate for such outcomes-based programs

Such an effort requires a coalition of the willing. For this voluntary project, the Education Department should tap high-quality providers like those profiled in chapter 4, open-minded financial aid experts, interested accreditors and perhaps other entities in the quality assurance world, and technology companies willing to help build the necessary systems.

Those of us who worked on the EQUIP program during the Obama administration saw firsthand how even a tiny experiment, with a belt-and-suspenders approach to safeguards, was fiercely opposed by traditionalists within the Education Department. When they lost that fight and EQUIP was approved as an experiment, it was opposed by allies in the White House Office of Budget Management. Then, when the pared-down version eventually made its way into the implementation phase, it took so long and became so complicated that the program was doomed to fail. No one was ill intended here—critics fervently believe in their approach and cite the many examples of shoddy programs operating behind the mask of innovation. The professionals at FSA, always understaffed and running a massive system, are tasked with risk mitigation, not innovation, and the culture is not designed for experiments such as EQUIP. A demonstration project to support new alternatives to time-based learning will need the full backing of leadership within the Education Department, who are willing to drive the execution of the project through the federal bureaucracy, inertia, and the inevitable resistance to innovation.

Policy follows practice. A demonstration project is a way for policy makers to learn from scores of high-quality competency-based programs that exist, many at scale, and to finally align our regulatory frameworks to better support those programs. Institutions can continue offering some or even most of their programs in the credit-hour system (or all of them if they wish) with an option of also offering some programs on a competency basis. But for those that take the leap, their students can enroll in programs that better recognize the knowledge and skills they already have, in addition to those they gain in their programs, while untethering them from the constraints of place and time. We could then have a system that pays for actual demonstrated learning instead of time served, that employers can trust, that supports students moving in and out of a learning ecosystem in the way that our modern work increasingly requires, and that invites innovation in delivery. As such programs proliferate, Americans will be much better able to get just the right skills they need at just the right time in just the right way, drawing down from a pool of financial aid dollars over the course of their lifetimes. It is easy to imagine subsequent policy and tax incentives for individuals and employers to add to that pool of dollars through lifelong learning accounts. This system would pay for performance, better protect taxpayer money, and distribute risk, while not requiring any more dollars than we already spend on higher education.

By focusing on the student and addressing the inequities of our time-based system, a competency-based demonstration project and the policies and systems that would follow its successful completion truly would be an innovation on the scale of the GI Bill, one for the American worker and every new generation trying to unlock opportunity and a shot at the American Dream. It could help us better understand and perfect a system that could eventually replace the increasingly antiquated, time-based system we built for the industrial age with one based on the outcomes we need for the digital age.

CHAPTER SIX

A BETTER FUTURE

I LOVE AMERICAN HIGHER EDUCATION. It transformed my life and the lives of my daughters. My entire career has been in this industry, which has given me joy, intellectual nourishment, community, admired colleagues, inspiring students, and a sense of meaning, maybe even a calling. It's easy for me to slip into nostalgia and wish we could go back to the version of higher education I first experienced in the 1970s. That was a system where a first-generation student like me could pay for college without taking on much debt, largely by working construction jobs in the summer and through work-study during the academic year. You also could expect to graduate and get a decent job.

That nostalgia comes with a couple problems. First, for all that worked well (and much did), I was still a white male. While I didn't *feel* privileged, higher education in the 1970s was an engine of social mobility better designed for someone like me than it was for large swaths of American society, especially communities of color. While colleges were

generally liberal in intellectual sensibilities, the racism and misogyny of
the time did not stop at the gates to campus. Second, higher education
as I experienced it was built for an industrial-age economy, not today's
technology-driven, globally connected world. Society is experiencing profound, often convulsive change. And our old systems, including higher
education, are not keeping up. The new technological age first disrupted
commerce, entertainment, and social networks. Now it's overtaking pol-
itics, finance, and the national discourse. In just one month in 2021, we
saw baseless conspiracy theories lead to insurrection and the storming
of the US Capitol, Reddit-organized day traders upend the stock market,
and the silencing of an outgoing US president as technology companies
like Twitter and Facebook decide whose voices get heard in our public discourse. In each case, our institutions and systems have struggled
to keep up.

The same is true for higher education. The industry was once respected
and commensurately supported for the ways it opened up opportunity,
created reliably skilled and capable workers, and was well aligned with
societal needs. Now it is seen as increasingly out of reach and out of touch
by students who struggle with the cost of college and question its return
on investment, by employers who can't get the workers they need and
no longer trust the quality of those they hire, and political leaders who
have reframed higher education as a personal interest rather than a public good as they accordingly reduce support. There is finger pointing in
every direction from stakeholders within higher education and its critics outside the industry. Administrators and boards decry faculty resistance to change and accountability. Faculty members cite administrative
bloat, inflated salaries, and the corporatization of their institutions, while
worrying about the fate of the liberal arts. Politicians seize on both while
engaging in culture wars and debates over political bias, correctness, and
speech. Consumer protection advocates bemoan the lack of quality control and the widespread abuses by bad for-profit players (and sometimes
by poorly performing nonprofits), which often have devastating financial
impacts on students. Government regulators want higher education to

do better, while higher education wants government to keep the money coming but to stay out of its business—a business that government often seems not to understand even while regulating it. Employers have millions of unfilled jobs but find that college graduates too often struggle to write well and lack other skills associated with a college degree, which was once a trustworthy signal to the labor market. Meanwhile, student debt mounts, college football coaches are the highest paid people in the industry, and institutional business models are deeply broken (as the credit ratings agencies have noted).[1] And after forty years of working to get more students across the finish line, college completion rates for society's bottom socioeconomic quartile have barely budged, even as the top two quartiles have seen significant gains.[2]

Higher education is leaving far too many people behind and is contributing to deepening socioeconomic inequity. The pandemic has laid bare that final, sad fact. The high-profile Varsity Blues college admissions scandal confirmed for many Americans what they had long suspected: that the game is rigged against lower-income students in higher education. They're not wrong. And a growing number of data points make clear that B-list celebrities fraudulently buying college slots for their under-qualified children is far from the only injustice in how selective four-year colleges admit students. Wealthy Americans with parents in the top 1 percent of earners are seventy-seven times more likely to attend an elite institution than their peers with parents in the bottom 20 percent of income, according to Harvard's Opportunity Insights.[3] And that gap appears to be growing. The Common Application, which is the most popular college application, reported in early 2021 that larger and more competitive institutions are doing well, with big jumps in applications.[4] Overall, applications in the US were up 10 percent. But the Common App found declines of two to three percentage points in applications from first-generation and lower-income applicants. The huge State University of New York and California State University systems, which enroll more lower-income students than virtually all other US universities, saw application declines of 20 percent and 5 percent, respectively.

Meanwhile, one in five community college students expects to delay their graduation because of the pandemic, according to a survey conducted in late 2020.[5] Even before the crisis, fewer than 40 percent of community college students earned a degree or certificate within six years of first enrolling—for programs that should take full-time students two years or less to complete.[6] Those odds are worse for Black and Latinx students. And for students who leave college without a credential, even a small amount of student loan debt can be catastrophic. More than one million borrowers default on their student loans each year, with the typical defaulter holding less than $10,000 in outstanding debt.[7] And nongraduates are three times more likely to default than borrowers who hold degrees.

This massive, complex, and regulated industry is not going to transform itself overnight. Yet higher education is broken and desperately needs rethinking, innovation, and courage. When something is broken, it's often most useful to drill down to the root causes or to return to fundamentals. The best coaches know that when a team is struggling, it is often time to get back to basics and build up from there. In the case of higher education, we need to get back to that most fundamental of functions, student learning. How we define it, how we assess it, how we structure it. As we have seen, the industry has been built around a deeply flawed artifact that was never intended for the uses to which it has been put: the credit hour. We now have something better: competencies. Competencies are transparent about claims for student learning, rigorous in the assessment of that learning, applicable to any discipline without dictating content or pedagogy, and applicable to ways of learning well outside the classroom or confines of the campus. They are building blocks that are more flexible and malleable in terms of designing programs better suited for various students and needs, that recognize what students already know, and that are responsive to the demands of the workforce and to society. Competency-based education can also provide more transparency, better quality, and a more efficient transfer credit system, as well as performance-based financial aid that is less prone to abuse and better designed for supporting learning across a lifetime.

Moving away from the credit hour makes all that possible, while removing from the equation constraints of time and its adverse impact on disadvantaged learners. Much has been made of getting more personalization into learning. Well, this is the most basic and powerful approach: let students determine the schedule and pace of their learning. When the pace and timing of learning are driven by individual student needs, a kind of magic happens. I've seen this magic firsthand with some of the most underserved learners possible who are enrolled in SNHU's competency-based programs.

"EMPOWERED TIMING"

Deadra is a twenty-four-year-old Black woman from Boston's Roxbury neighborhood who had tried the local community college, worked full time at UPS, and was the full-time guardian of her goddaughter. She says:

> *The self-paced aspect was great. The main thing was not feeling pressure to do school on a certain schedule. Sometimes I just couldn't do school and that was okay, I could check in with a coach to help me adjust my schedule. It was much better than feeling rushed to turn in work on a schedule when I had life happen. Every day is not the best day for school. I liked that it was on my time. I could sign in when I felt like I wanted to sign in.*

Karla is a thirty-nine-year-old immigrant from Brazil. She enrolled at community college but started a family and took a full-time, lower-level job at a technology company. She says:

> *The time was the biggest thing. I just couldn't do in-person classes because of the schedule and the family. My life schedule just didn't fit into the rigid schedule of traditional college. I liked it [the self-paced aspect of the program]. I was able to log in at midnight if that was the best time for me. Or spend all day on a Saturday. Or take a day off from work if I wanted to really catch up. It's just very straightforward.*

You don't have to spend time doing stuff you don't need. When I was in community college I had to sit through a whole semester doing algebra to take more advanced math courses that I was able to do just as easily. This was just right to the point.

Luis is a twenty-nine-year-old Black man who works full time in a social service agency, had tried college before, and has a three-year-old son. He says:

When I graduated from high school I was always home with both my parents and I didn't like being away from home. It was hard. I was so involved with my family. So I came back. But then I started working and attending community college and the rigid schedule was too much to handle. Things happen. If I have to cancel the time with SNHU/ Duet, I just reschedule. Even if it's at the last minute, it's okay. I like that you're not rushed—there are no deadlines. I have a three-year-old I take care of, so when I can't do school or need to take a week off, I'm under no pressure with a deadline and I can catch up. I lost my mom at twenty-three, and I've been the head of household with my little brothers, so for a long time for me it has been job first. And you just can't be job first in most schools.

Franklin is a twenty-six-year-old Rwandan refugee who resettled in the Boston area and previously attended community college in Maine. He says:

The traditional course-based model took too long to take one course. You could never get ahead. You had to wait for everyone else to come up. I was working, so [with SNHU/Duet] I could do my schoolwork on my schedule in a way that met my needs. In the traditional model I needed to set my own personal schedule to the scheduling needs of the institution.

Did this flexibility around time mean these students would be delayed or slow to complete their studies? It was quite the opposite. With the academic coaching and support of our delivery partner, Duet, and newfound flexibility around time, their pace was actually quicker than normal. Deadra earned her associate *and* bachelor's degrees in just 2.5 years. Karla earned her associate degree in two years (well ahead of the national average of 5.6 years, particularly impressive for a student who worked full time) and is now pursuing her bachelor's degree.[8] Luis completed his associate degree in two years and has started his bachelor's degree. Franklin finished his associate and bachelor's degrees in just two years. Skeptical of the quality of a degree earned that quickly? Franklin is on his way to Harvard Business School.

Mike Larsson, the cofounder and president of Duet, is thoughtful about the ways in which time-bound systems of education might have thwarted these enormously talented students from earning a degree:

> *Work, life, and cost were enormous barriers because traditional college is draconian. Miss a couple of weeks in October because your mom is sick? College is over, or at least seriously hampered. Owe $97? Can't enroll. Can't access your transcripts for any class you've ever passed. Job changed your hours in February and now you can no longer attend your English class? Sorry. You need to drop out. Also, your Pell Grant is cancelled. And since the federal government isn't paying for this class, you owe us.*
>
> *Life happens, interferes, and changes what's possible for our students. But with College for America, your college changes with you. So if that means you need to take two weeks off to take care of your mom, that's okay. And if it means you want to do schoolwork every day and get your degree in one year because you get a raise as soon as you get a degree, that's okay too.*
>
> *Also, as we look at alumni—the self-paced aspect allows students to see success, to feel success, and to see how their effort in time will tie directly into how fast they'll earn a degree. It's an enormously powerful motivator for students as they still have to sacrifice free time and stay up late and miss weekend events to earn that degree.*

When we think about scarcity in underserved communities, we rightly think about money. Poverty has a direct impact on the most basic needs, including food and housing, and on the basics of life in a modern economy, such as access to computing and connectivity (an inequity of access that the shift to remote learning during the pandemic vividly revealed). As a result, poverty draws heavily from everyone's standard time bank of the twenty-four-hour day—everything just takes longer—and allows less flexibility in how that time can be used. By adhering to time as a building block of learning and to rigid schedules for study, traditional higher education disadvantages low-income students and contributes to inequity.

The impact of time and its scarcity on learning is perhaps nowhere more severe than for refugee learners. Starting in 2017, SNHU's Global Education Movement (GEM) program has worked on the world's most ambitious attempt to bring full degree programs to refugee learners. It operates in camps in Rwanda, Malawi, and Kenya, as well as with refugee populations in South Africa and Lebanon. (While we often think of camps when we think of refugees, 70 percent of displaced people are dispersed in host communities.) For a refugee, much of the day can be consumed with the most basic life-sustaining functions, like procuring water, cooking fuel, and food rations, and navigating the endless demands of paperwork and bureaucracy that are often imposed on refugees. For example, one of our staff members accompanied Latetia, a GEM student in Cape Town, South Africa, to have her asylum papers renewed, a task she had to do every six months. The line that stretched around the block had already started to form when they arrived at 7 a.m. When officials closed the office nine hours later, Latetia had not yet made it inside the building and had to return the next day, starting all over again. In Kakuma Camp in Kenya, Jimmy, another SNHU student, routinely waits four hours in over one-hundred-degree heat for food rations and then walks ninety minutes back home, using much of his twenty-four-hour time bank for something you or I might spend thirty minutes on, if we haven't had groceries delivered straight to our home. Chrystina Russell, who leads GEM, says:

SNHU's direct-assessment, competency-based model has turned time upside down in higher education at a level that parallels the time drained for individuals living in poverty. By untethering the credit hour from seat time, students are able to face the daunting challenges of time scarcity while also tackling a degree. The fact that there are no due dates and that the schedule is 100 percent driven by students rather than the institution flips the power dynamic of time for students. Where they usually have demands on time and little to no control or say as to when a meeting might be with a humanitarian, government, or other organization, SNHU places the power directly in their hands. While it takes some discipline and practice to effectively wield this time-empowered gift, students usually learn to manage this somewhat unexpected (and often unpracticed) power. The result is being able to meet the time demands of poverty and earning a degree. What SNHU has done—offering empowered timing—is the single most powerful component of its innovation for refugee learners, in my opinion. It is higher ed's most powerful response to a core structure and system destroying the lives of those living in poverty.

While the plight of global refugees, an admittedly extreme case, illustrates the inequity that time-based education models impose on underserved populations, it is not so far removed from the realities of low-income people in this country. When Arne Duncan, the former US Secretary of Education and a member of the GEM Advisory Board, saw the power of removing time from the learning equation, he commented to me, "If it can work in Rwanda and Lebanon, it should work on the south side of Chicago." SNHU's competency-based program is now part of Duncan's Chicago CRED program, which combats gun violence through job training, education, and support programs aimed at those mostly likely to be caught up in Chicago's deadly cycles of gang and gun violence.

Disconnecting from time allows more creativity in how to construct academic programs. For example, competency-based programs often have much more flexibility about when students begin and end their learning. Russell recounts this exchange in a New York Supreme Court courtroom when Tomas (not his real name), a seventeen-year-old former student of hers, was facing a prison term. She was advocating for him to instead be allowed to enroll in our program.

> JUDGE: *This sounds promising, but I don't see how it's going to work. It's April. Are we going to have him in Rikers for another five months before the school year starts?*
>
> PROSECUTOR: *Agreed, and he cannot be out doing no program until September, so unfortunately, I don't think this is a viable option.*
>
> TOMAS'S ATTORNEY: *I've been informed that Tomas can start this month, or any subsequent month as long as his paperwork is in by the twentieth of the previous month. Judge, Tomas can start as soon as he is released from Rikers if we decide this is the best pathway forward.*
>
> JUDGE: *I'm sorry, he can start at the beginning of each month? That's highly unusual How can I confirm this?*

The judge only knew the traditional September and January start times for conventional college programs. Tomas might have been just another statistic in the school-to-prison pipeline, serving five to nine years in prison and carrying a criminal record with him for the rest of his life, with all the detrimental impacts that go with it. Instead, he completed his associate degree, has started his bachelor's degree, and walks through the world as a college student instead of walking around a prison yard as a felon. It is tempting to suggest that competency-based education is an exceptional model for people in exceptionally bad circumstances. But a better way to frame its strength is to evoke universal design. For example, curb cuts in sidewalks were designed for people with disabilities, but they made everyone's walk down the street better—older people, little kids, and parents pushing baby carriages, and anyone who might have stepped off a curb and inadvertently turned an ankle. What works so well for refugees and a kid looking at prison might actually work for any busy learners who are juggling work, family, and their studies (the majority of today's college students), particularly those from low-income backgrounds.

CHANGING MINDSETS AND LIVES

When we can design around actual learning and not time, we invite the kind of innovation and development of new delivery models that higher education and so many students desperately need right now. When we start looking at measurable outcomes to define quality, we can overcome our fixation with dubious and often expensive signals of quality that drive up college costs and fuel the race for status. It's a shift that will make many uncomfortable. My colleagues often complain in private about the excesses of their high-profile football or basketball programs, but also delight in the glamour, spotlight, and status of "owning" a nearly professional sports franchise that millions watch on television every week. Luxury dorms, food courts, and signature architecture are markers of prestige, but they don't mean much if student outcomes are poor. For faculty members across much of higher education, accountabilities will shift from articles published, books written, conference presentations given, and governance committees attended to measures of student learning, teaching performance, and to some extent, job placement and graduation rates. Of course, research institutions play other critically important roles in our higher education system, engaging in basic research and knowledge making, and we need them to be well supported and robust in those functions. Though they, too, would have to rein in misplaced fixations with football and trophy buildings.

Higher education is full of people who care deeply about students. But our institutions and much of our industry spend too much of their time and focus on matters other than student learning. By and large, higher education looks at student performance as a reflection of student ability rather than the learning model, its delivery, instructor effectiveness, and design. The greatest challenge to widespread adoption of a competency-based education model might be that it demands more of everyone—institutions, faculty, and students. Our current system of higher education, still largely centered on campus-based education and measures of time, is failing. Forty percent of students who start a four-year degree program will not have completed after six years.[9] We graduate large numbers of students who slide by with as little work as possible and enter the workforce deficient in basic knowledge and skills. Grades are inflated and tell us little in most cases. The overall system is financially unsustainable, and is either out of reach for too many or saddles them with debilitating debt.

Proposals for free college or debt forgiveness, rooted in the admirable desire to make college work for underserved students, subsidize but don't fix the problem. They help, but the result is like cleaning up pollution downstream while the factory upstream continues to put chemicals in the river. We need to get at the root cause, to create a new model for education. That is harder, more complex, and takes longer. Shifting to competencies as a basis for learning, allowing students to go as fast or as slow as they need to master the knowledge and skills required of them, will ask much of us. Perhaps too much, at least all at once:

- We will see even more clearly than we do now the degree to which public K–12 education is sending students to higher education who are ill prepared for college-level work.
- We will remove the traditional status markers so deeply ingrained in the higher education system—inputs such as buildings, amenities, endowment, and reputation—and replace them with transparent outputs: clearly stated claims for what students know and can do and rigorous assessments that reassure us they work. For many institutions, we will finally see if the emperor has clothes.
- For faculty, the good news is that competency-based education does not require them to change their pedagogy, the way they like to teach. In fact, because this approach to learning focuses on competencies and rigorous performance-based assessments, we actually open up possibilities for almost any kind of pedagogy that works. Nothing about competency-based education dictates or prescribes pedagogical approach—as long as the student masters the required competencies, it doesn't matter how they got there. The challenge for faculty is this:

- When faculty design a course, they will have to be clear about the claims they make for students' knowledge and skills in ways that have rarely been demanded of them in the past.
- They will need to rethink their assessment practices, which are often weak.
- The new level of transparency will make clear how well they have done in educating their students.
- While competency-based education allows for new high-quality, shorter sub-degree programs, and learning that is recognized from noncollege sources, the industry will work hard to protect its monopoly on what counts as postsecondary learning.

Perhaps most untenable, we may see graduation rates fall, at least for some time. The reason is that, on one hand, rigorous assessment and genuine mastery of knowledge and skills are a lot harder than the current implicit pact that often asks too little of students, inflates grades, and thus requires less of faculty and institutions. On the other hand, it's unacceptable that 40 percent of students who start in our current system never complete. And we know the design and cost of this system shut out far too many people, especially those who are low income and live in marginalized communities.

Taken together, these recommendations for change are probably a bridge too far for the industry. Also, too much that is genuinely good about higher education might be placed at risk if we forced a sudden and dramatic shift to a completely competency-based education system.

So, the ask here is for something more modest. It is to create a safe space for innovation and learning to take place, to create a Plan B for those institutions willing to raise their hands and design new outcomes-based programs for students who want and need them. Because higher education is so regulated, inventing this new alternative approach also needs the willingness and courage of regulators and accreditors to allow and support the effort. A demonstration project of the kind proposed in chapter 5 can provide the regulatory space in which to try this alternative approach.

Institutions like the ones described in chapter 4 would need to step forward. Political leaders and government appointees will have to push through the bureaucratic inertia and risk aversion of the US Department of Education. A modern technology company like Salesforce or Google might be needed to build the required platform for dispersing financial aid in a new way. And maybe even more important than the players and actions needed will be the mindset required to reinvent higher education in this way. That's because this is disruptive, which means we will get some things wrong and will need to commit to learning quickly and making adjustments. What we create will not be wanted or accepted by many students (maybe even most) for some time. Like all disruptive innovations, these models will be adopted first by students at the margins— those refugee learners and students with severe time scarcity—because disruptive innovations always take hold first with those whom the incumbent industry does not serve well. However, don't underestimate the millions of students who live on those margins.

As competency-based education improves, employers will start gravitating toward graduates of programs whose assessments of student learning they trust; students will find lower-cost alternatives and exciting new ways to learn, unburdened by the constraints of time and place; and higher education will be revitalized and renewed for the age in which we live. The benefits are myriad:

- We will make learning once again the nonnegotiable core of American higher education and the building block of our systems, processes, and institutional structures.
- We will encourage all kinds of new learning models, because in a world where outcomes are most important, we can embrace almost any approach that produces the desired outcomes.
- Because the quality of learning will be well understood and measurable, those new models will innovate around the cost of delivery and price to students.
- The federal financial aid system will start paying for actual performance rather than time served, with inherent incentives for

improved completion rates and an institutional focus on student success.

- Employers will be able to move from assessing graduates' learning based on the vague outline that is a transcript and the unreliable grades it reports to transparent measures of what students know and can do, backed up by rigorous assessments.

- We will be able to build learning and credentials of greater granularity, provided by a wider range of players, opening our learning ecosystem to provide students with more options across their careers. Meanwhile, improved approaches to quality assurance, built-in caps on access to financial aid, and risk sharing will provide much better protections against abuse than our current regulatory frameworks.

- The humanities, long in decline, will have a stronger case to make for itself, especially as algorithms replace technical work and distinctly human skills like critical thinking, meaning making, design, and human interaction—the enduring skills rightfully associated with the humanities—become more in demand.

- We will be able to achieve the long-sought alignments of K–12 with higher education (as K–12 itself moves toward competency frameworks) and of higher education with work. We will be able to make those pipelines coherent and efficient in ways that elude us today.

Online education began in a demonstration project, became better and better over the years as we learned more, was accessed by millions of students and available at almost every institution by 2019, and then saved the industry when the COVID-19 pandemic hit. When we emerge from the pandemic, higher education will be weakened, and all the issues that pushed the industry toward its current crisis will be amplified and accelerated.

Perhaps a crisis is required to break the hold of time, inputs, status seeking, and cost on an industry that cannot fix itself with incremental tweaks and belt tightening. It has taken the existential threat of climate catastrophe to finally begin to shake the hold of the fossil-fuels industry. As the threat sinks in, the world's largest car manufacturer, General

Motors, has announced it will not produce gasoline-powered vehicles by 2035. Coal production is down 50 percent over the last decade, while solar power has grown 45-fold during the same time period.[10] The Biden administration has proposed a green energy plan framed as a job-creation engine while recognizing climate as a security threat. My own university offsets almost all its power use through purchase agreements for renewables and has a plan to be genuinely climate neutral by 2030. Moving away from a carbon-based energy infrastructure will require a massive shift in infrastructure and advances in technology, creating winners and losers. Elon Musk, founder of electric car manufacturer Tesla, is now the first or second wealthiest man in the world. His car company, which first made a profit in 2020, is valued at more than GM, Ford, and Fiat Chrysler combined. Most importantly, attitudes have shifted, and 77 percent of Americans now say we must prioritize the development of renewable energy. The race to avert climate catastrophe and the embrace of a viable Plan B could not happen without such a change in mindset.

Almost everything we need in order to offer a different form of higher education, an alternative to our incumbent and failing system, is available to us today. This vision can be realized. Many questions certainly remain unanswered, with a corresponding number of details to be sorted out. But infrastructure and frameworks are being developed, as are basic nomenclature and taxonomies (in the world of microcredentials, for example). Areas of particular weakness in our current system, such as assessment, will require enormous work. And I saw firsthand the fierce resistance to change and fear of innovation that dogged even a modest proposal like EQUIP. The pushback from entrenched interests that would seek to undermine a fundamental rethinking of higher education will be substantial— maybe the most formidable hurdle we face. But the oil and gas industry is hardly letting go easily either, and we can't shirk from taking on either challenge.

When we get it right—and it will take years—American higher education can once again lead the world, creating opportunity for people, developing a twenty-first-century workforce, driving social mobility, lifting the underserved, providing an intellectual bulwark against misinformation and demagoguery, and giving its graduates the tools to thrive in a complex and fast-changing world full of wonder and dread. We are going to need such people if we are to reverse America's decline. A country that once defeated the Nazis, put humans on the Moon, invented the Internet, and declared a war on poverty now struggles to protect elected officials and the institutions of democracy from white nationalists and neo-Nazis; has lost more lives to COVID-19 than in World War I, World War II, the Korean War, and the Vietnam War combined; sees one-third of GoFundMe campaigns for uninsured medical costs; and accepts that more than 27 percent of households with children struggle to get enough to eat.[11]

Nelson Mandela famously said, "Education is the most powerful weapon which you can use to change the world." To my mind, higher education has two fundamental jobs:

- to create the new knowledge, basic research, and breakthroughs that deepen our understanding of the world and fuel human progress
- to unlock opportunity and social mobility to allow people to improve their lives and the lives of their families and communities

This book is about the latter purpose, about the challenge of transforming the lives of those people who are increasingly being left behind in an inequitable economic system where disparities of opportunity are reinforced by hierarchies of race and class. If we are to fix a broken America, we cannot afford to squander the talent and intelligence that is as abundant in our poorest communities, our rural towns and underserved urban neighborhoods, as it is in wealthy, privileged enclaves.

Before the pandemic, I spent a couple of hours on a playground in a Los Angeles neighborhood beset by gangs and suffering one of the highest murder rates in the city. I was there with our partners at the Da Vinci Schools, which were using our competency-based program with homeless kids. The playground was their classroom. A gifted Da Vinci science teacher was teaching thermodynamics and scientific methods with the humblest of tools available to her: Cheetos and Bic lighters. She had the kids burn the Cheetos, record their observations on clipboards, and then discuss what they recorded, what they theorized was happening, and how they might then test those hypotheses. Watching them work and listening to their discussion, I observed students as curious, intelligent, and engaged as those in my daughters' well-resourced high school. In many ways they were far more impressive because of what they had to overcome in their daily lives to be on that playground. The students highlighted throughout this book remind us that talent is universally distributed, but opportunity is most emphatically not. For these students, we need a new American higher education.

Every year I stand on stage, shake the hands of graduates, and pass them diplomas as they have their moment in the spotlight. Some bound up the stage pumping fists, some carry a child in their arms, and others wear a ribbon signifying their military service. I often find those seconds together quite moving. At a graduation in 2019, one of the students I knew from our competency-based program stood at the bottom of the stairs. His face was serious as he nervously awaited his name. I knew the student's story. He had been in and out of public housing, was trying to be father to his child despite the lack of role models in his own life, and had just barely avoided being pulled into local gangs, the only employers who were hiring in his community. His name was called, and he arrived at center stage to receive his diploma. As we shook hands, he leaned in and whispered in my ear, "Thank you. You saved my life." That is the higher education I want for America.

NOTES

PREFACE

1. Stephanie Owen and Isabel Sawhill, *Should Everyone Go to College?* (Washington, DC: Center on Children and Families at Brookings, 2013), https://www.brookings.edu/wp-content/uploads/2016/06/08-should-everyone-go-to-college-owen-sawhill.pdf.

2. "Buyers Beware," Georgetown University Center on Education and the Workforce, https://cew.georgetown.edu/cew-reports/collegemajorroi/.

3. Matt Reed, "Friday Fragments," *Inside Higher Ed*, December https://www.insidehighered.com/blogs/confessions-community-college-dean/friday-fragments-193.

4. Goldie Blumenstyk, "By They Said 2 out of 3 Jobs Would Need More Than a High-School Diploma. Were They Right?" *Chronicle of Higher Education: The Edge*, January https://www.chronicle.com/newsletter/the-edge/2020-01-22.

5. Beth Bean, Andrew Hanson, and Michelle Weise, "The Permanent Detour," Strada Education Network, https://stradaeducation.org/report/the-permanent-detour/.

6. Paul Beaudry, David A. Green, and Benjamin M. Sand, "The Great Reversal in the Demand for Skill and Cognitive Tasks," National Bureau of Economic Research, March https://www.nber.org/papers/w18901.

7. Jason DeParle, "Harder for Americans to Rise from Lower Runs," *New York Times*, January https://www.nytimes.com/2012/01/05/us/harder-for-americans-to-rise-from-lower-rungs.html?auth=link-dismiss-google1tap.

8. "First Year Experience, Persistence, and Attainment of First-Generation College Students," Center for First-Generation Student Success, https://firstgen.naspa.org/files/dmfile/FactSheet-02.pdf.

9. Eduardo Porter, "In Public Education, Edge Still Goes to Rich," *New York Times*, November https://www.nytimes.com/2013/11/06/business/a-rich-childs-edge-in-public-education.html?partner=rss&emc=rss&smid=tw-nytimes.

10. Tami Luhby, "Many Millennials Are Worse Off Than Their Parents—A First in American History," CNN, January https://www.cnn.com/2020/01/11/politics/millennials-income-stalled-upward-mobility-us/index.html.

11. Jeffrey M. Jones, "Confidence in Higher Education Down since 2015," Gallup, October https://news.gallup.com/opinion/gallup/242441/confidence-higher-education-down-2015.aspx.

12. "Fulfilling the American Dream: Liberal Education and the Future of Work," Association of American Colleges and Universities, https://www.aacu.org/research/2018-future-of-work.

13. "How Can We Amplify Education as an Engine of Mobility," Opportunity Insights, https://opportunityinsights.org/education/.

14. Isabel Sawhill and Katherine Guyot, *The Middle Class Time Squeeze*, (Washington, DC: Economic Studies at Brookings, August 2020), https://www.brookings.edu/wp-content/uploads/2020/08/The-Middle-Class-Time-Squeeze_08.18.2020.pdf.

CHAPTER 1

1. "Survey Reveals Gap Between Public and Policymakers When It Comes to Understanding Today's College Students," *Higher Learning Advocates*, October https://higherlearningadvocates.org/news/survey-reveals-gap-between-public-and-policymakers-when-it-comes-to-understanding-todays-college-students-2/.

2. "College Student Employment," National Center for Education Statistics, last modified May https://nces.ed.gov/programs/coe/indicator_ssa.asp.

3. "Types of Aid," Federal Student Aid, https://studentaid.gov/resources/types-infographic-accessible.

4. Amy Laitinen, *Cracking the Credit Hour* (Washington, DC: New America Foundation and Education Sector, 2012), https://static.newamerica.org/attachments/2334-cracking-the-credit-hour/Cracking_the_Credit_Hour_Sept5_0.ab0048b12824428cba568ca359017ba9.pdf.

5. Laitinen, *Cracking the Credit Hour*, 6.

6. *Transfer & Mobility: A National View of Student Movement in Postsecondary Institutions, Fall Cohort* (Herndon, VA: National Student Clearinghouse Research Center, 2015), https://nscresearchcenter.org/wp-content/uploads/SignatureReport9.pdf.

7. Michael B. Horn and Richard Price, "Higher Ed's Credit Transfer System Is Broken. Here's a Better Way," *EdSurge*, April https://www.edsurge.com/news/2020-04-20-higher-ed-s-credit-transfer-system-is-broken-here-s-a-better-way.

8. Scott Jaschik, "Pressure on the Provosts," *Inside Higher Ed*, January https://www.insidehighered.com/news/survey/pressure-provosts-2014-survey-chief-academic-officers.

9. Richard Arum and Josipa Roksa, *Academically Adrift* (Chicago: University of Chicago Press Books, 2010).

10. Todd Rose, *The End of Average* (New York: HarperOne, 2015).

11. Rose, *The End of Average*, 133.

12. Rose.

13. Laitinen, *Cracking the Credit Hour*, 10.

14. "Program Integrity Questions and Answers—Credit Hour," US Department of Education, https://www2.ed.gov/policy/highered/reg/hearulemaking/2009/credit.html.

15. Laitinen, *Cracking the Credit Hour*.

16. Rebecca Klein-Collins et al., *The PLA Boost* (Indianapolis, IN: CAEL & WICHE: 2020), 51–https://www.cael.org/hubfs/PLA%20Boost%20Report%20CAEL%20WICHE%20-%20October%202020.pdf.

17. Dallas Kratzer, Louis Soares, and Michele Spires, *Recognition of Prior Learning in the 21st Century* (Boulder, CO: ACE & WICHE: 2021), https://www.wiche.edu/wp-content/uploads/2021/02/ACE-brief-020821.pdf.

18. Clayton M. Christensen and Henry J. Eyring, *The Innovative University: Changing the DNA of Higher Education from the Inside Out* (San Francisco: Jossey-Bass, 2011).

19. Steven Brint, "Is This Higher Education's Golden Age?," *The Chronicle of Higher Education,* January https://www.chronicle.com/article/is-this-higher-educations-golden-age/.

20. Matt Richtel, "How the Pandemic Is Imperiling a Working-Class College," *New York Times,* December https://www.nytimes.com/2020/12/28/us/college-coronavirus-tuition.html.

21. Jennie H. Woo et al., *Repayment of Student Loans as of Among 1995–and 2003–First-Time Beginning Students* (Washington, DC: National Center for Education Statistics, 2017), https://nces.ed.gov/pubsearch/pubsinfo.asp?pubid=2018410.

22. Gregor Aisch et al., "Some Colleges Have More Students from the Top 1 Percent Than the Bottom Find Yours," *New York Times,* January https://www.nytimes.com/interactive/2017/01/18/upshot/some-colleges-have-more-students-from-the-top-1-percent-than-the-bottom-60.html.

23. *Populace Insights: American Priorities for Higher Education* (Burlington, MA: Populace Inc., 2020), https://static1.squarespace.com/static/59153bc0e6f2e109b2a85cbc/t/5f09ce581207ba5845a1821d/1594478170087/Populace+Higher+Education+Index.pdf.

24. *Report on the Economic Well-Being of U.S. Households in* (Washington, DC: Board of Governors of the Federal Reserve System, 2019), https://www.federalreserve.gov/publications/files/2018-report-economic-well-being-us-households-201905.pdf.

25. "News & Announcements," The Carnegie Classification, https://carnegieclassifications.iu.edu/.

26. "VALUE," Association of American Colleges & Universities, https://www.aacu.org/value.

27. Ken Robinson, *Out of Our Minds: The Power of Being Creative* (Chichester, UK: Wiley, 2017).

28. *Findings from the National Survey of Postsecondary Competency-Based Education* (Washington, DC: American Institute for Research & Encoura Eduventures Research, 2019), https://www.air.org/sites/default/files/National-Survey-of-Postsec-CBE-2018-AIR-Eduventures-Jan-2019.pdf.

29. "Capella University Fact Sheet," Capella University, last modified November https://www.capellaresults.com/content/dam/capella/PDF/FactSheet.pdf.

30. "Gartner Hype Cycle," Gartner, https://www.gartner.com/en/research/methodologies/gartner-hype-cycle.

CHAPTER 2

1. "Southern New Hampshire University," Fast Companies, https://www.fastcompany.com/company/southern-new-hampshire-university.

2. Clayton M. Christensen, *The Innovator's Dilemma* (New York: McGraw-Hill, 1997).

3. Paul LeBlanc, "Online Learning and Civic Engagement," *Southern New Hampshire University, President's Corner,* May https://president.snhu.edu/2014/05/online-learning-and-civic-engagement/.

4. Scott Jaschik, "Obama vs. Art History," *Inside Higher Ed,* January https://www.insidehighered.com/news/2014/01/31/obama-becomes-latest-politician-criticize-liberal-arts-discipline.

5. Aamer Madhani, "Obama Apologizes for Joking About Art History Majors," *USA Today,* February https://www.usatoday.com/story/theoval/2014/02/19/obama-apologizes-to-texas-art-history-professor/5609089/.

6. David Deming, "In the Salary Race, Engineers Sprint but English Majors Endure," *New York Times,* September https://www.nytimes.com/2019/09/20/business/liberal-arts-stem-salaries.html.

7. Mark Schneider and Matthew Sigelman, *Saving the Liberal Arts* (Washington, DC: American Enterprise Institute and Burning Glass Technologies, February 2018), https://www.burning-glass.com/wp-content/uploads/Saving-the-Liberal-Arts.pdf.

8. Education Department, "Notice Inviting Postsecondary Education Institutions to Participate in Experiments Under the Experimental Sites Initiative; Federal Student Financial Assistance Programs Under Title IV of the Higher Education Act of as Amended," *Federal Register,* October https://www.federalregister.gov/documents/2015/10/15/2015-26239/notice-inviting-postsecondary-educational-institutions-to-participate-in-experiments-under-the.

9. "What Is New Collar?," IBM Training, https://www.ibm.com/training/newcollar.

10. Paul Fain, "IBM Looks Beyond the College Degree," *Inside Higher Ed,* October https://

www.insidehighered.com/digital-learning/article/2019/10/29/interview-ibm-official-about-companys-new-collar-push-look.

11. Glassdoor Team, "More Companies That No Longer Require a Degree—Apply Now," *Glassdoor,* January https://www.glassdoor.com/blog/no-degree-required/.

12. Executive Office of the President, "Executive Order Modernizing and Reforming the Assessment and Hiring of Federal Job Candidates," June https://www.federalregister.gov/documents/2020/07/01/2020-14337/modernizing-and-reforming-the-assessment-and-hiring-of-federal-job-candidates.

13. Jennifer Arnold, "How to Adopt Skills-Based Hiring Practices," *SHRM,* February https://www.shrm.org/hr-today/news/hr-magazine/0318/pages/hiring-for-skills-not-pedigree.aspx.

14. *A Survey of Displaced Workers and Online Learning Experiences: Initial Insights* (Manchester: Southern New Hampshire University, 2020).

15. "About Us," Credential Engine, https://credentialengine.org/about/.

CHAPTER 3

1. Doug Lederman, "Harsh Take on Assessment . . . From Assessment Pros," *Inside Higher Ed,* April https://www.insidehighered.com/news/2019/04/17/advocates-student-learning-assessment-say-its-time-different-approach.

2. Wolfgang Stroebe, "Why Good Teaching Evaluations May Reward Bad Teaching: On Grade Inflations and Other Unintended Consequences of Student Evaluations," *Perspectives on Psychological Science* no. 6 (2016): 800–16.

3. Molly Worthen, "The Misguided Drive to Measure 'Learning Outcomes,'" *New York Times,* February https://www.nytimes.com/2018/02/23/opinion/sunday/colleges-measure-learning-outcomes.html.

4. "Air Traffic Control Specialists," Federal Aviation Administration, last modified October https://www.faa.gov/jobs/career_fields/aviation_careers/.

5. Jennifer Kite-Powell, "Exploring New Worlds in Virtual Reality," *ASU News,* December https://news.asu.edu/20201222-creativity-exploring-new-worlds-virtual-reality.

6. Ray Schroeder, "Vaccinate Against Cheating with Authentic Assessments," *Inside Higher Ed,* February https://www.insidehighered.com/digital-learning/blogs/online-trending-now/vaccinate-against-cheating-authentic-assessment.

7. "Employers Want to See These Attributes on Students' Resumes," *NACE,* December https://www.naceweb.org/talent-acquisition/candidate-selection/employers-want-to-see-these-attributes-on-students-resumes/.

8. "Guidelines on Competency-Based Theological Education (CBTE)," Association of Theological Schools, April https://www.ats.edu/uploads/accrediting/documents/guidelines-for-cbte-programs%20%2815%20April%202020%29.pdf.

9. "Decades of Scientific Research That Started a Growth Mindset Revolution," Mindset Works, https://www.mindsetworks.com/science/; "Martin E. P.

Seligman," Positive Psychology Center, https://ppc.sas.upenn.edu/people/
martin-ep-seligman.

CHAPTER 4

1. "Nation's Top 'Best Value' Colleges of Education Announced by National Council
   on Teacher Quality," National Council on Teacher Quality, September https://
   www.nctq.org/dmsView/Best_Value_Campaign_Press_Release_(with_Link).
2. *Moving Competency-Based Education Forward* (Minneapolis, MN: Capella University and Whiteboard Advisors, n.d.), https://www.capella.edu/content/
   dam/capella/PDF/moving-competency-based-education-forward.pdf.
3. Christina Amato and Nancy Thibeault, "CBE: Ready, Set, Go Competency-Based Education Model," Sinclair Community College, March https://
   ohiocommunitycolleges.org/wp-content/uploads/2016/11/CBE-Ready-Set-Go-
   Thibeault-Amato-Sinclair-Community-College.pdf?x57939.
4. *WGU Alumni Outcomes Report Great Jobs, Great Lives—Gallup Study of Recent
   Western Governors University Alumni* (Washington, DC: WGU and Gallup,
   2018), https://www.wgu.edu/content/dam/web-sites/mvp/global/reports/gallup-
   report-2018.pdf.
5. Genevieve Kirch, letter to WGU President Robert W. Mendenhall, November
   https://archive.wgu.edu/system/files/artifact-files/20001125%20-%201%20
   want%20to%20express%20my%20deepest%20gratitude.pdf.
6. *WGU Annual Report* (Salt Lake City, UT: WGU, 2019), https://www.wgu.edu/
   content/dam/western-governors/documents/annual-report/annual-report-
   2019.pdf.
7. Paul Fain, "Efficiency, at Scale," *Inside Higher Ed,* October https://www
   .insidehighered.com/news/2016/10/18/competency-based-educations-business-
   model-offers-promise-report-finds.
8. John Gravois, "The College For-Profits Should Fear," *Washington Monthly,* Sep-
   tember/October https://washingtonmonthly.com/magazine/septoct-2011/the-
   college-for-profits-should-fear-2/.
9. Alexandra Pannoni and Emma Kerr, "Everything You Need to Know About
   Community Colleges: FAQ," *U.S. News & World Report,* July https://www
   .usnews.com/education/community-colleges/articles/2015/02/06/frequently-
   asked-questions-community-college.
10. "Table 503.Percentage of to 64-year-old undergraduate students who were
    employed, by attendance status, hours worked per week, and selected char-
    acteristics: and 2017," National Center for Education Statistics, https://nces
    .ed.gov/programs/digest/d18/tables/dt18_503.40.asp.
11. *Accelerating Pathways to Careers for Adult Learners* (Washington, DC: Jobs for
    the Future, n.d.), https://files.eric.ed.gov/fulltext/ED603652.pdf.
12. "Earn Credit for Your Experience," Lipscomb Online, https://www.lipscomb
    .edu/online/admissions/earn-credit-your-experience.

13. Melinda Karp, "First-Year Momentum—What It Is and Why It Matters," *Student Success Network*, http://csustudentsuccess.net/2019/01/first-year-momentum-what-it-is-and-why-it-matters/.
14. Van Davis, "New Regulations Review #Regular and Substantive Interaction," WCET Frontiers, April https://wcetfrontiers.org/2020/04/03/new-regs-review-1-regular-substantive-interaction/.
15. Peter Greene, "Is Competency-Based Education Just a Recycled Failed Policy," *Forbes*, October https://www.forbes.com/sites/petergreene/2018/10/08/is-competency-based-education-a-recycled-failed-policy/?sh=38347135dfc5.
16. Robert Shireman, "The Real Value of What Students Do in College," *The Century Foundation*, February https://tcf.org/content/report/the-real-value-of-what-students-do-in-college/.

CHAPTER 5

1. "Applying for Title IV Eligibility for Direct Assessment (Competency-Based) Programs," Federal Student Aid, March https://ifap.ed.gov/dear-colleague-letters/03-19-2013-gen-13-10-subject-applying-title-iv-eligibility-direct-assessment.
2. Zarmina All, "The World's Largest Banks, 2020," S&P Global Market Intelligence, April https://www.spglobal.com/marketintelligence/en/news-insights/latest-news-headlines/the-world-s-100-largest-banks-2020-57854079.
3. Kaitlin Mulhere, "Congress Just Made It a Lot Easier to Apply for Financial Aid," *Money*, December https://money.com/fafsa-simplification-pell-grants-spending-bill/.
4. Bill Gates, "Fixing Financial Aid," *Gates Notes*, May https://www.gatesnotes.com/Education/Fixing-financial-aid.
5. Delece Smith-Barrow, "A Worrying Trend This Fall: Decline in FAFSA Applications," *Hechinger Report*, November https://hechingerreport.org/a-worrying-trend-this-fall-decline-in-fafsa-applications/.
6. "Current Term Enrollment Estimates," National Student Clearinghouse Research Center, December https://nscresearchcenter.org/current-term-enrollment-estimates/.
7. "High School Benchmarks with a COVID-Special Analysis," National Student Clearinghouse Research Center, December https://nscresearchcenter.org/high-school-benchmarks/.
8. "Point of View: The Whole U.S. Economy Was like a Giant Pre-existing Condition," *Jobs for the Future*, June https://www.jff.org/points-of-view/brookings-institution-senior-fellow-and-jff-board-member-richard-v-reeves-in-6-insights-that-could-make-economic-recovery-more-equitable-this-time/.
9. "Public Viewpoint: COVID-Work and Education Research," Strada Center for Education Consumer Insights, January https://cci.stradaeducation.org/public-viewpoint/.

10. *C-BEN Quality Assurance Review Process* (Franklin, TN: Competency-Based Education Network, 2019), https://www.cbenetwork.org/wp-content/uploads/2020/06/CBEx-19-035-Quality-Assurance-Doc-WEB.pdf.

11. "Generation Z Views Traditional College Path as Old School," ECMC Group, https://www.ecmcgroup.org/news-generation-z-views-traditional-college-old-school.html.

12. "Public Viewpoint: COVID-Work and Education Research."

13. Andrew Kreighbaum, "Brewing Battle over Pell Grants," *Inside Higher Ed*, July https://www.insidehighered.com/news/2019/07/08/debate-over-proposed-expansion-pell-grants-short-term-job-training.

14. Wesley Whistle, "Short Memories Lead to Long-Term Consequences," New America, Last modified January https://www.newamerica.org/education-policy/reports/short-memories-lead-long-term-consequences-higher-education-policy/.

15. John Richards and Chris Dede, "The 60-Year Curriculum: A Strategic Response to a Crisis," Educause Review, October https://er.educause.edu/articles/2020/10/the-60-year-curriculum-a-strategic-response-to-a-crisis.

16. Jamie Merisotis, *America Needs Talent* (New York: RosettaBooks, 2015).

17. *The LiLA Demonstration After Four Years: A Summary of Public Policy Associates' Second Interim Evaluation Report on the Lifelong Learning Account Demonstration Program* (Indianapolis, IN: Council for Adult and Experiential Learning, 2007), http://publicpolicy.com/wp-content/uploads/2017/04/CAELsummary LiLASecondInterimReport.pdf.

18. SkillsFuture Singapore, https://www.skillsfuture.gov.sg/.

19. "Lifelong Learning Accounts," Washington Workforce Training and Education Coordinating Board, https://www.wtb.wa.gov/planning-programs/past-workforce-projects/lifelong-learning-accounts/.

20. *Short-Term Programs in the Shadows* (Oakland, CA, and Washington, DC: The Institute for College Access and Success, 2019), https://ticas.org/wp-content/uploads/2019/08/short-term-programs-in-the-shadows.pdf.

21. "Accreditation in the United States," US Department of Education, https://www2.ed.gov/admins/finaid/accred/accreditation_pg6.html.

22. Doug Lederman, "More Than Bridgepoint on Trial," *Inside Higher Ed*, March https://www.insidehighered.com/news/2011/03/11/more-bridgepoint-trial.

23. Ivy Bridge University v. Higher Learning Commission, (Cal. 2015), https://www.insidehighered.com/sites/default/server_files/files/2015-05-14%20 Complaint.pdf.

24. Paul Fain, "Something Has to Give," *Inside Higher Ed*, July https://www.insidehighered.com/news/2012/07/06/accreditation-crisis-hits-city-college-san-francisco.

25. "Pelosi, Speier, Eshoo Condemn Continued ACCJC Failure of Leadership in CCSF Matter," Congresswoman Nancy Pelosi, May https://pelosi.house.gov/

news/press-releases/pelosi-speier-eshoo-condemn-continued-accjc-failure-of-leadership-in-ccsf-matter.

26. Paul Fain, "Trouble for an Accreditor," *Inside Higher Ed,* August https://www.insidehighered.com/news/2015/08/31/californias-community-colleges-may-seek-new-accreditor.

27. Paul Fain, "City College of San Francisco's Severe Budget Crisis," *Inside Higher Ed*, January https://www.insidehighered.com/quicktakes/2020/01/23/city-college-san-franciscos-severe-budget-crisis.

28. Susan D. Phillips and Kevin Kinser, *Accreditation on the Edge: Challenging Quality Assurance in Higher Education* (Baltimore: John Hopkins University Press, 2018).

29. Danielle Douglas-Gabriel, "Education Dept. Staff Recommends Dropping Embattled For-Profit-College Accreditor Backed by DeVos," *Washington Post,* January https://www.washingtonpost.com/education/2021/01/22/acics-education-department-recognition/.

30. Phillips and Kinser, *Accreditation on the Edge,* viii.

31. Katie Lannan, "Mass. Commission Adopts New Rules for College Closures," WBUR, January https://www.wbur.org/edify/2020/01/10/massachusetts-college-closure-regulations.

32. "National Council for State Authorization Reciprocity Agreements (NC-SARA), NC Sara, https://nc-sara.org/.

33. Patricia A. Wood, "The U.S. Department of Education and Student Financial Aid for Distance Education: An Update. ERIC Digest," EricDigests.org, February https://www.ericdigests.org/2002-2/distance.htm.

34. Ben Miller, "How For-Profits Lost Their Way," *Inside Higher Ed,* May https://www.insidehighered.com/views/2014/05/30/profit-colleges-went-astray-should-return-their-roots-essay.

35. Sophie Quinton and National Journal, "Will a For-Profit Degree Get You a Job?" *Atlantic,* March https://www.theatlantic.com/politics/archive/2014/03/will-a-for-profit-degree-get-you-a-job/430758/.

36. *For Profit Higher Education: The Failure to Safeguard the Federal Investment and Ensure Student Success* (Washington, DC: United States Senate, Health Education, Labor, and Pensions Committee, 2012), https://www.help.senate.gov/imo/media/for_profit_report/PartI.pdf.

37. Kevin Carey, "Proposed Merger Blurs the Line Between For-Profit Colleges and Public Universities," *New York Times,* August https://www.nytimes.com/2020/08/11/upshot/university-of-arizona-ashford-zovio-online-college.html.

38. "IRS and Education Could Better Address Risks Associated with Some For-Profit College Conversions," GAO Highlights, December https://www.gao.gov/assets/720/711600.pdf.

CHAPTER 6

1. "NCAA Salaries," NCAA, https://sports.usatoday.com/ncaa/salaries/; Rick Seltzer, "Rating Agencies Issue Dour Higher Ed Outlook for Next Year," *Inside Higher Ed*, December https://www.insidehighered.com/quicktakes/2020/12/09/rating-agencies-issue-dour-higher-ed-outlook-next-year.

2. Richard Whitmire, "Alarming Statistics Tell the Story Behind America's College Completion Crisis: Nearly a Third of All College Students Still Don't Have a Degree Six Years Later," *The* April https://www.the74million.org/article/alarming-statistics-tell-the-story-behind-americas-college-completion-crisis-nearly-a-third-of-all-college-student-still-dont-have-a-degree-six-years-later/.

3. "How Can We Amplify Education as an Engine of Mobility," Opportunity Insights, https://opportunityinsights.org/education/.

4. Scott Jaschik, "'Alarm Bells' on First-Generation, Low-Income Applicants," *Inside Higher Ed*, January https://www.insidehighered.com/admissions/article/2021/01/26/common-apps-new-data-show-overall-gains-applications-not-first.

5. "Public Viewpoint: COVID-Work and Education Research," *Strada Center for Education Consumer Insights*, January https://cci.stradaeducation.org/wp-content/uploads/sites/2/2021/01/Report-January-27-2021.pdf.

6. Elizabeth Mann Levesque, "Improving Community College Completion Rates by Addressing Structural and Motivational Barriers," *Brookings*, October https://www.brookings.edu/research/community-college-completion-rates-structural-and-motivational-barriers/.

7. Elissa Nadworny, "These Are the People Struggling the Most to Pay Back Student Loans," *NPR*, July https://www.npr.org/2019/07/09/738985632/these-are-the-people-struggling-the-most-to-pay-back-student-loans.

8. "Time to Degree—2016," *National Student Clearinghouse Research Center*, September https://nscresearchcenter.org/signaturereport11/.

9. "Graduation Rates," National Center for Education Statistics, https://nces.ed.gov/fastfacts/display.asp?id=40.

10. Drew Desilver, "Renewable Energy Is Growing Fast in the U.S. but Fossil Fuels Still Dominate," *Pew Research Center*, January https://www.pewresearch.org/fact-tank/2020/01/15/renewable-energy-is-growing-fast-in-the-u-s-but-fossil-fuels-still-dominate/.

11. Christianna Silva, "Food Insecurity in the U.S. by the Numbers," *NPR*, September https://www.npr.org/2020/09/27/912486921/food-insecurity-in-the-u-s-by-the-numbers/.

ACKNOWLEDGMENTS

THIS BOOK BEGAN WITH A CALL from Nancy Walser, my initial editor at Harvard Education Press. Bridget Terry Long, dean of the Harvard Graduate School of Education (and gracious writer of the foreword to this book), had interviewed me on her podcast, and Nancy was listening that day and reached out to ask if I had considered a book. I had, but it was Nancy who persuaded me it was time to actually start writing, who guided me through the initial stages of the work, and who was enormously patient when I diverted from my original target date. She retired and handed off this project to her colleague, Jayne Fargnoli, who brought it the rest of the way home. Jayne's enthusiasm for the book and expert shepherding were of enormous help.

Bridget's role in this book did not end with that initial conversation. After I had completed the draft, I wanted a foreword that would place the book in a broader context, in this extraordinary moment in time, and written by someone who cares as much about equity, genuine learning, and students as I do. Bridget graciously agreed to take on the task, for which I am enormously grateful.

Help came from many other sources, and my circle of readers provided feedback, suggestions, and questions that made this book better than it would have been if left wholly in my hands. Included in that group are Barbara Brittingham, Michael Horn, Charla Long, Amy Laitinen, Maria Flynn, Matt Wunder, Mike Larsson, Kemp Battle, Will Pena, Tim Lehman, Lauren Starks, Pat Findlen, and Emma and Hannah LeBlanc. They didn't always agree with the analysis or arguments I was putting forth (some disagree still), but they were all generous with their time, with their thoughtful comments and suggestions, and their encouragement. Jackie Lavorgna was an expert researcher throughout, chasing down information for me and making sure we properly documented our sources.

Clay Christensen, my dear friend of nearly forty years, has intellectual fingerprints all over this book, though he passed away before seeing it come to print. Clay served on the SNHU board, often wrote about our innovation story, and was a wise counselor and warm hearted friend. He was among the greatest of teachers, a good man that I miss very much.

There have been many fine teachers along the way. The ones who directly changed my life, people like Mark Schlafman, Elizabeth Collins, Helen Heinemann, Alan Feldman, Charlie Moran, and Anne Herrington. The best learning comes when we are surrounded by people who believe in us and challenge us to be better, as I learned from those gifted teachers. Colleagues can also be teachers—the best are co-learners—and I have had a great many. In doing the work in competency-based education that informs so much of the book, I was joined by Yvonne Simon, Martha Rush-Mueller, Brian Peddle, Kate Kazin, Kris Clerkin, and a great many others.

I learn every day from my talented colleagues on my leadership team at SNHU, some who have been by my side for well over a decade. The SNHU innovation story is as much theirs as mine—more really, because they make it happen day in and day out. The SNHU Board of Trustees are not in the day-to-day work, but they are stewards of the "big" vision and among my most valuable thought partners. In my SNHU role, I have found community and calling among colleagues who deeply care about the students being left behind.

I am endlessly grateful to Paul Fain, one of the very best journalists in our industry. In a bit of fortuitous timing, he left his position at *Inside Higher Ed* at the end of 2020 and was available to help with the book in the first two months of 2021, when the really heavy lift occurred; he was invaluable. Paul is an excellent editor, improved my writing, and was a thought partner as much as an editor. Putting his reporter's skills to good use, he conducted most of the interviews that inform our short case studies and provided student perspectives. Paul is a friend, an expert writing partner, and one of the best people in higher education—someone who wants it to be better because he cares about it so much.

We both were inspired by students throughout the writing of this book, as I have been for all of my career. Whether online, on campus, in a refugee camp, working with one of our partners, deployed overseas, or behind prison walls, students overcome so much to make better lives for themselves and their families. They deserve the best higher education system possible. I have more than four decades of students in my life, many of whom I stay in touch with today, and more often than they knew, I was the student learning from them.

I had additional help in final editing from my daughter Emma, an excellent writer and exacting editor who did not let familial ties stand in the way of necessary feedback and much improved prose. She and her sister Hannah have now surpassed their father in most ways, and I often stand in awe of their fierce intellects, sense of social justice, and grace. They also make me laugh more than anyone but their mother, from whom they inherited all their best traits (well, maybe not their height— that one I claim). Pat has for years urged me to write this book. She read drafts, asked good questions, made suggestions, and was supportive of the hours and weekends stolen for this project, offering only encouragement and an occasional cup of tea and a power bar on long writing days. These three powerhouse women in my life are my compass, my map, and my safe, loving harbor.

ABOUT THE AUTHOR

DR. PAUL J. LEBLANC is President of Southern New Hampshire University (SNHU). Under the eighteen years of Paul's direction, SNHU has grown from 2,800 students to more than 170,000 and is the largest non-profit provider of online higher education in the country, and the first to have a full competency-based degree program untethered to the credit hour or classes approved by a regional accreditor and the US Department of Education.

In 2012 the university was number twelve on *Fast Company* magazine's "World's Fifty Most Innovative Companies" list and was the only university included. *Forbes Magazine* has listed Paul as one of its fifteen "Classroom Revolutionaries" and one of the "most influential people in higher education" for 2016, and *Washington Monthly* named him one of America's ten most innovative university presidents. In 2018, Paul won the prestigious IAA Institute Hesburgh Award for Leadership Excellence in Higher Education, joining some of the most respected university and college presidents in American higher education.

He has served on the Board of the American Council on Education, the Association of Governing Boards President's Council, the Academy of Sciences Board on Workforce and Higher Education, as well as many others. He is a sought-after speaker, often appears in the media, and is a contributing writer to Forbes Magazine.

INDEX

as disruptive innovation, 44–47, 165
massively open online courses, 32–33
at Southern New Hampshire University, 3
state licensure and, 145
Open University, 91–92
opportunity versus talent, 168
outcomes movement, 115, 142
outcomes versus inputs, 15–17, 39, 89–91. *See also* competency-based higher education
Out of Our Minds (Robinson), 30

paper-and-pencil tests, 67
Pell Grants, xvii, 5, 122, 126, 131–132
performance. *See* competency-based higher education
performance-based assessments
development of, 71–73
early education example, 83–84
examples of, 75–78
faculty resistance to, 69–73
value of, 70–71
Phillips, Susan, 140, 141–142
PLA (prior learning assessment), 13–14, 90, 105, 109, 131. *See also* competency-based higher education
plateau of productivity, 32–33
pluggability, 62
Populace, 19–20, 61
positive feedback, 110
poverty. *See* income level
power distribution, 82
power skills, 29–30
Price, Richard, 8
prior learning assessment (PLA), 13–14, 90, 105, 109, 131. *See also* competency-based higher education
privilege, benefitting from, 151–152

program design
accountability versus freedom, 113–116
Lipscomb University, 104–108
Northern Arizona University, 108–113
overview, 89–95
Salt Lake Community College, 103–104
Sinclair Community College, 101–102
Southern New Hampshire University, 92–95
Western Governors University, 95–100

R2T4 (Return to Title IV), 129
race, cost-shifting and impacts of, 18–19
Reeves, Richard V., 123
refugee learners, 158–159
"regular and substantive" interaction requirement, 111
reliability in assessment, 66–67
residential colleges, as exception to the norm, 2
reskilling, 60, 132
resubmissions, 21, 50, 75, 86–87
Return to Title IV (R2T4), 129
reverse engineering, 74–75, 80–81, 89, 99, 110. *See also* program design
Robinson, Ken, 30
Romer, Roy, 96
Rose, Todd, 10–11
rubrics, 49–50, 77–78
Russell, Chrystina, 158–159, 160

Salt Lake Community College (SLCC), 103–104, 124
Schlafman, Mark, xvi
school-to-prison pipeline, 160
Schroeder, Ray, 73